LOVE V. REGENCY

Second Edition

Love v. Regency

Edward Stein, JD

and

Jonathan Rest, MD

NATIONAL INSTITUTE FOR TRIAL ADVOCACY

Address inquiries to:

Reprint Permission
National Institute for Trial Advocacy
1685 38th Street, Suite 200
Boulder, CO 80301-2735
Phone: (800) 225-6482
Fax: (720) 890-7069
Email: permissions@nita.org

ISBN 978-1-60156-706-2
eISBN 978-1-60156-705-5
FBA 1706

Printed in the United States of America

Official co-publisher of NITA.
aspenpublishing.com/NITA

CONTENTS

EXHIBITS

APPENDICES

Acknowledgements

We would like to extend many thanks to Ann Arbor, Michigan, lawyer Larry Jordan for his help on IT issues. Another thank you goes to Paul Zwier of Emory Law School and Frank Rothschild of Kauai, Hawaii, for their help on many issues. This case file wouldn't be the same without their help.

The National Institute for Trial Advocacy wishes to thank Facebook for its permission to use likenesses of its website as part of these teaching materials.

CASE SUMMARY

Dr. Stanley Love is a Central City dermatologist who, for more than a decade, has performed cosmetic surgery, in addition to his general dermatology practice. Since YR-13, he has marketed his cosmetic surgery practice with "The Love Look" as his slogan. Dr. Love did not register the slogan with any state agency or with the U.S. Patent and Trademark Office.

In mid-YR-13, two New York City plastic surgeons formed Regency Plastic Surgery, PC. In YR-12, Regency registered the service mark "The Look of Love" with the U.S. Patent and Trademark Office, and began using the slogan in all its marketing. Over the years, Regency expanded its market area when it purchased plastic surgery practices in communities beyond New York City.

In YR-6, Regency purchased a plastic surgery practice in Oakdale, a well-to-do bedroom community located twenty-five miles north of Central City, and began using "The Look of Love" in its marketing campaign in the Central City area. Central City has a population of about 750,000. The metropolitan area has a population of about 1,400,000.

In early YR-1, Dr. Love filed suit against Regency, alleging infringement of his common law trademark of "The Love Look," seeking injunctive relief and damages. Regency denies liability, claiming that Dr. Love had no common trademark because "The Love Look" is merely descriptive and, therefore, Dr. Love could acquire no common law trademark rights in the slogan. Regency also claims that, even if "The Love Look" has acquired trademark protection, Regency did not infringe the trademark. Finally, Regency claims that Dr. Love's claims are barred by laches and the statute of limitations.

A summary of the applicable law is at pages 123-124.

INSTRUCTIONS FOR USE
AS A FULL TRIAL

1. The plaintiff and the defendant must call the two witnesses listed as that party's witnesses on the witness list.

2. All witnesses can be played by any gender.

3. All witnesses called to testify who have identified the parties, other individuals, or tangible evidence in statements or prior deposition testimony must, if asked, identify the same at trial. Additionally, witnesses have knowledge of all documents on which their signatures appear.

4. Each witness who testified previously agreed under oath at the outset of his or her testimony to give a full and complete description of all material events that occurred and to correct the transcript of such testimony for inaccuracies and completeness before signing the deposition transcript.

5. All exhibits in the case file are authentic. In addition, each exhibit contained in the file is the original of that document unless otherwise noted on the exhibit or as established by the evidence.

6. All signatures are authentic. No advocate may attempt to impeach a witness by arguing that a signature on a transcript, statement, or exhibit does not comport with a signature or initials on an exhibit.

7. Other than what is supplied in the problem itself, there is nothing exceptional or unusual about the background information of any of the witnesses that would bolster or detract from their credibility.

8. The case file is a "closed universe" of facts, and competitors may use only the materials in the file except where the file states otherwise.

9. "Beyond the record" shall not be entertained as an objection. Rather, advocates shall use cross-examination to impeach the witness regarding any material facts not contained in the case file. Where asked, witnesses must admit that the fact to which they have testified is not in their statement or testimony.

10. The Statement of the Case shall not be used as evidence or for examination or cross-examination of any witness.

PROCEDURAL MATTERS

11. Federal Rules of Evidence and Federal Rules of Civil Procedure apply.

12. The trial may relate to liability only or liability and damages. Verdict forms are provided for both.

13. All dispositive pretrial motions have been filed and denied; no further dispositive motions (other than Motions for Judgment as a Matter of Law) will be entertained.

SUBSTANTIVE MATTERS

14. The parties stipulate that the State of Nita has jurisdiction over this matter. No issues of jurisdiction or venue are pertinent to the case at hand.

OTHER INSTRUCTIONS

15. All years in these materials are stated in the following form:

     a.   YR-0 indicates the actual year in which the case is being tried (i.e., the present year);

     b.   YR-1 indicates the next preceding year (please use the actual year);

     c.   YR-2 indicates the second preceding year (please use the actual year), etc.

16. The applicable law is contained in the case law and proposed jury instructions set forth at the end of this case file.

17. Electronic copies of all exhibits, deposition videos, and the accompanying PowerPoint presentation can be found at the following website:

                            http://bit.ly/1P20Jea
                            Password: Love2

STATE COURT OF NITA
COUNTY OF NITA

STANLEY LOVE, MD and STANLEY LOVE, MD, PC,	)	
	)	
	)	
Plaintiffs,	)	
	)	
vs.	)	CIVIL NO. YR-1–CV–96369
	)	
REGENCY PLASTIC SURGERY,	)	
	)	
Defendant.	)	
	)	

COMPLAINT AND JURY DEMAND

The plaintiffs for their complaint against the defendant allege:

1. Plaintiff, Stanley Love, MD ("Dr. Love"), is a resident of this State, and is the sole owner of plaintiff, Stanley Love, MD, PC, a professional corporation.

2. Dr. Love is a board-certified dermatologist and a trained cosmetic surgeon who practices dermatology and cosmetic surgery in the Central City area.

3. Defendant, Regency Plastic Surgery, PC, is a New York corporation that is authorized to do business in this State.

4. Starting in YR-13, and continuing to date, Dr. Love has used the phrase "The Love Look" in marketing his cosmetic surgery practice in the Central City area.

5. By virtue of his use of "The Love Look," Dr. Love and/or his PC acquired common law trademark rights to "The Love Look" in connection with cosmetic surgery services in this State.

6. Starting in YR-6 and continuing to date, Regency has used the phrase "The Look of Love" to market its cosmetic surgery services in the Central City area.

7. Regency's use of "The Look of Love" infringes on plaintiffs' trademark rights to "The Love Look."

8. Plaintiffs have been damaged by defendant's infringement in an amount equal to plaintiffs' resultant lost income, or defendant's wrongful profit, whichever is greater.

9. Plaintiffs are entitled to treble damages because defendant's infringement has been, and continues to be, willful.

WHEREFORE, plaintiffs request:

a. Damages in the amount of plaintiffs' loss or defendant's profit, whichever is greater; and

b. That plaintiffs' damages be trebled; and

c. A permanent injunction against defendant's use of "The Look of Love."

PLAINTIFFS demand trial by jury.

Filed: 01/04/YR-1

SCHMIDT, WARREN & ROTHSCHILD by:

Carl Schmidt

Carl Schmidt
400 S. Ashley Street
Central City, Nita 80144

STATE COURT OF NITA
COUNTY OF NITA

STANLEY LOVE, MD, et al.,	)	
	)	
Plaintiffs,	)	
	)	
vs.	)	CIVIL NO. YR-1–CV–96369
	)	
REGENCY PLASTIC SURGERY,	)	
	)	
Defendant.	)	
	)	

ANSWER

1. Neither admitted nor denied.

2. Neither admitted nor denied.

3. Admitted.

4. Neither admitted nor denied.

5. Defendant denies that "The Love Look" is subject to plaintiffs acquiring any common law trademark rights because the phrase is merely descriptive of surgery performed by Dr. Stanley Love.

6. Defendant acknowledges that since YR-6, it has made lawful use of its registered service mark, "The Look of Love®", in marketing its plastic surgery services in the Central City area.

7. Denied.

8. Denied.

9. Denied.

AFFIRMATIVE DEFENSES

1. The six-year statute of limitations has expired on some or all of plaintiffs' claims.

2. Plaintiffs' claims are barred by the doctrine of laches.

3. Plaintiffs have infringed defendant's registered service mark and, therefore, come to court with unclean hands.

WHEREFORE, defendant requests that this Court dismiss plaintiffs' Complaint with prejudice, and award costs to defendant.

Defendant demands trial by jury.

Filed: 02/12/YR-1

KILPATRICK, STONE & SHAH by:

Alicia Robertson

Alicia Robertson
1400 Vernor Ave.
Central City, Nita 80144

STATE COURT OF NITA
COUNTY OF NITA

STANLEY LOVE, MD, et al.,   )
)
Plaintiffs,   )
)
vs.   )   CIVIL NO. YR-1–CV–96369
)
REGENCY PLASTIC SURGERY,   )
)
Defendant.   )
)

ANSWERS TO PLAINTIFFS' INTERROGATORIES AND REQUESTS FOR ADMISSIONS [excerpted]

Plaintiffs' Interrogatories to Defendant

Interrogatory #8: Please provide the name and address of all Regency Oakdale patients who obtained from Regency Oakdale the cosmetic surgery procedures listed on Exhibit 3, indicating for each patient, which procedure(s) he/she obtained and the date(s) thereof.

Response #8: Defendant declines to respond and objects to this interrogatory because the information sought is privileged and confidential pursuant to federal law (HIPAA) and state law providing for physician–patient privilege.

Plaintiffs' Requests for Admission

Request #3: Please admit that a pre-existing State common law trademark takes precedence, in this State, over a trademark that is later registered with the U.S. Patent and Trademark Office.

Response #3: Admitted

Depositions

STANLEY LOVE, MD
JAN. 9, YR-0

1   My name is Stanley Love, MD. I'm fifty-five years old. I graduated from Northern Illinois

2   University in YR-35, and the University of Illinois School of Medicine. I did my dermatology

3   training at the University of Michigan, after which I started working for Dr. Eric Brown.

4   That's when we first moved to Central City. When Eric retired about twenty years ago,

5   I took over his practice and incorporated it. The corporate name is Stanley Love, MD, PC.

6   I've been in practice by myself ever since then. I am board certified in dermatology, and

7   I'm a fellow of the American Society of Cosmetic Surgery. No, I don't teach at any medical

8   school. No, I'm not board certified in cosmetic surgery.

9

10 For the first ten years, my practice was very much like most derm practices. I did some

11 surgery—biopsies and excisions and that kind of thing—but I mostly I did general

12 dermatology. But my favorite part has always been the surgery. I'm pretty good at it.

13

14 In the summer of YR-15, I took a course in eyelid surgery. After this, I started doing eyelid

15 surgery as a part of my practice. I took some more courses in cosmetic surgery over the next

16 several months, and as I started doing more and more surgery in my practice, I began to get

17 referrals from my primary care friends, specifically for cosmetic surgery. No, I didn't have

18 cosmetic surgery training as a part of my residency. But I understand that derm residents do

19 get training in cosmetic surgery these days—eyelid surgery, Botox, liposuction. Even facelifts.

20 And the seminars I attended were all accredited by the American Academy of Cosmetic Surgery.

21

22 At the time, my wife, Bobbi, who is also my office manager, encouraged me to do more

23 cosmetic surgery. She used to joke with my patients. When they'd come into the office,

24 she'd ask them if they'd come for the "Look of Love." We decided it would be great to get

25 more cosmetic surgery patients, and my wife talked to a friend who runs the ad agency

26 downstairs in our building—it's called the Gamble Agency. He agreed to help us advertise

27 the practice. No, we don't have a formal contract with Gamble. Ed Gamble warned us that,

1 because "The Look of Love" was a song title, there might be legal problems in using it in

2 our advertising. So we changed it to "The Love Look."

3

4 So we came out with a brochure in the spring of YR-13. And it has that logo on the front

5 page—"The Love Look"—along with my picture. Yes, Exhibit 2 is the version of the brochure

6 we've been using since about YR-4. Also in YR-13, we started to put ads in the paper. At first

7 they were small, but by the end of the year, we were taking out one-eighth-page ads. And

8 then in YR-8, we started to advertise on cable TV. We considered radio, but Ed Gamble

9 promised more bang for our buck if we went with cable TV. He recommended that I be in

10 the commercials myself. So we decided to go for it.

11

12 I remember the first time we filmed one of those commercials. I was so nervous, I was

13 shaking like a leaf … but it turned out to be no big deal. And then we did some more,

14 and I got to like it. I was pretty good at it. We've made six or eight since we began. Now,

15 new patients come in asking for the "Love Look." I remember the first time I heard it in

16 public. Bobbi and I were at one of our favorite restaurants, and the couple at the next

17 table—they were discussing cosmetic surgery. And the wife said that she wanted to go in

18 for the "Love Look." We laughed at the time, but it became a really big deal. No, we never

19 registered the slogan with the Patent and Trademark Office. We didn't know anything

20 about that. No, the Gamble people never mentioned anything about registering.

21

22 The TV ads made a big difference. A lot more cosmetic surgery patients came in. Before

23 we started doing the TV ads, we used to see one or two new cosmetic surgical patients

24 per week. By the end of YR-8, I had at least three times that many. That's new patients.

25 And they came in for the big procedures right off the bat. Blephs—that's eyelid surgery to

26 remove the sag—and Botox and lipo. It was a big success. Those ads were so successful

27 that early in YR-7, we decided to stop the newspaper ads and focus on TV.

28

29 I do a lot of cosmetic procedures, including blepharoplasty, dermabrasion, filler injections

30 like collagen, sclerotherapy, laser resurfacing, chemical peels, liposuction, and Botox.

1 I hope to introduce mini-facelifts within the next year. As I said, my training for all of these

2 procedures has been through the Cosmetics Institute. They're a training center in Chicago.

3 They offer all kinds of procedure workshops, which are approved by the American Academy

4 of Cosmetic Surgery. I do most of these procedures in my office, though I do have privileges

5 at the Central City Surgi-Center. It's been a while since I did a case at the Surgi-Center. I'd

6 have to check my records to be sure. But, I occasionally do go there. For example, if I have

7 an elderly patient, and I want to have a nurse anesthetist with me when I operate, then I'll

8 go to the Surgi-Center.

9

10 On September 4, YR-6, one of my patients told me about Regency. I remember the

11 conversation as if it were yesterday. It was the day before my birthday. I was looking for

12 a chart in the file, and I heard my wife greet one of our regular patients on the phone

13 with a joke about our TV commercial, which she often did, and the patient wanted to

14 make an appointment in our new Oakdale office. That stopped me dead in my tracks. My

15 wife told her that we don't have an office in Oakdale, which is twenty-five miles north of

16 Central City. That we have only the one office. She said that she had seen an ad in Central

17 City Monthly for our Oakdale office. She was sure it was us because the ad used my name

18 and slogan.

19

20 My wife and I looked on the internet right after work that afternoon. We Googled

21 Oakdale and The Love Look and found a paid ad for Regency. When we clicked on the

22 link we discovered "The Look of Love" and come to find out that it was Drs. Connelly

23 and Waters—two surgeons in Oakdale that I've known for a long time. They used to do

24 mostly reconstructive work, and a lot of burns. But now they're a part of Regency, and

25 they're using a slogan that is almost identical to ours. And they're only doing cosmetics.

26 Yes, I know they're not dermatologists. They're plastic surgeons, but my patient certainly

27 didn't know that. As a matter of fact, she didn't even make an appointment with us that

28 day. She said she would call back, but she didn't. Anyway, as you can imagine, I was very

29 concerned about what I found out about Drs. Waters and Connelly. I didn't sleep very well

30 that night.

1	Q.	Did you do anything to express your concerns to Dr. Waters or Dr. Connelly?
2		
3	A.	Yes, of course.
4		
5	Q.	What did you do?
6		
7	A.	I called Dr. Waters three times over the next few days, but he never called
8		me back.
9		
10	Q.	What messages did you leave him?
11		
12	A.	I just asked him to call me back.
13		

14 When he didn't, I called my lawyer, John Dixon, to ask what I should do. He suggested that

15 I write a letter to Regency, and ask them to stop using the slogan. I thought maybe they

16 didn't even realize what they were doing, although in retrospect? They knew full well what

17 was going on. So on September 13, I wrote a letter to Dr. Segan, the President of Regency.

18 I asked her to stop using the "Look of Love" slogan. Yes, Exhibit 3 is the letter I wrote

19 her. Unfortunately, it didn't do any good. She wrote me back in October, but she said they

20 wouldn't stop using the slogan. She said it wouldn't make any difference because they

21 don't advertise on TV. She told me I shouldn't worry, because they didn't plan to steal any

22 of my derm patients. But that's rubbish. They've been stealing my patients ever since.

23

24 My income has fallen substantially because of Dr. Segan and Regency. At least 30 percent.

25 In YR-6, my cosmetic surgery revenue was over $325,000. Last year it was about $250,000.

26 I'm certain that difference is attributable to a decrease in the number of cosmetic

1 procedures I've been doing since Regency came to town. Yes, Exhibit 4 is the record of my

2 cosmetic procedures from YR-8 through YR-1. We enter each procedure I perform and the

3 actual income we receive. We enter the data into a program called Medisoft, which is a

4 standard medical-financial program. The program generated the report. Our bookkeeper

5 does the actual inputting and she gets the program to generate whatever kind of report

6 we need. No, I don't use the program myself, but I know it's been quite reliable, and that

7 many doctors use it.

8

9 I've had several patients ask me if I was working with the Regency doctors. They thought

10 that since they were using the Look of Love slogan, that we must be affiliated with them

11 somehow. I even had to put a sign up in the office informing my patients that we had

12 nothing to do with Regency. A lot of our patients are still very confused about that.

13 Yes, some of our patients have told us that they called Regency by mistake. To make

14 appointments. They said that when they called, Regency gave them our phone number.

15 They had it right there ready to give to our patients when they called. Can you imagine?

16 They've known all along that they were causing all this confusion, and yet they continue

17 to use our slogan.

18

19 Exhibit 10 is a printout of my website homepage. I had Ed Gamble add the warning that I'm

20 not associated with any other medical practice right after I got Dr. Segan's letter blowing

21 off my concerns.

22

23 In late YR-2, I met a woman at a charity event who told me that she meant to have eyelid

24 surgery done by me, but, because of her confusion over Regency's ads she made an

25 appointment there instead, and wound up having the surgery done there. And she was

26 very disappointed with the results.

1   Q.   When did you first consider suing Regency?

2

3   A.   In the spring three years ago. Ed Gamble told me that, if he were me, he'd

4   sue. I thought long and hard about it, but I decided not to.

5

6   Q.   Why?

7

8   A.   Because I don't like the idea of people suing each other, and I thought I could

9   probably ride out the economic impact. But after my income kept on going

10   further and further down, I didn't really have much choice, did I?

11

12 Yes, I'll tell you what the "Love Look" is all about. It's about common sense. When my

13 patients come in for the "Love Look" they know they're getting the surgery that's right for

14 them. They know I'm not going to sell them a bill of goods just to get a surgical fee. I give

15 them my promise that what I do will really make a difference in their lives. And they know

16 that if I don't think the surgery is right for them, I won't do it. I have a book filled with

17 letters from my cosmetic patients, thanking me for what I did. Word of mouth is really my

18 best advertising. The "Love Look" is about trust—their trust in me, and my good name.

19

20 No, I don't have any specific retirement plans. I love what I do, and I plan to keep doing it

21 as long as I can. At some point, I suppose, I might hire an associate to cut down my time in

22 the office a little. Yes, I'd like eventually to sell my practice to someone. That would provide

23 retirement income.

24

25 I have read the foregoing, and it an accurate transcription of my deposition testimony

26 given on Jan. 9, YR-1.

Stanley Love, MD

CATHERINE DELP
JAN 11, YR-0

1   I'm Catherine Delp. I'm forty-six years old, and I live at 1407 Whitehall Road in Oakdale.

2   I'm the CFO of Homes Are Us, which is the largest residential real estate agency in this

3   area. I have a bachelor's degree from Penn State and an MBA from Central City State. I'm

4   married and I have two sons, one in high school and one in college.

5

6   Dr. Love is my cosmetic surgeon. He's performed eyelid surgery, and I get regular Botox

7   injections from him. I first saw him in YR-4. After thinking about cosmetic surgery for

8   a couple of years, I finally decided to look into it. I'd seen Dr. Love on television, and he

9   seemed like a very nice man, and a friend of mine had gone to him and really liked him.

10   Then I saw an ad in Central City Monthly for what I thought was Dr. Love's Oakdale office,

11   and I called and made an appointment.

12

13   I thought the ad was for Dr. Love because it used his name, and it was for cosmetic surgery,

14   and so I assumed it was Dr. Love. Exhibit 8 is either the ad I saw, or something very

15   much like it. Yes, the ad said "Regency Plastic Surgery," which I assumed it was Dr. Love's

16   business's name.

17

18   Q.   Did you specifically ask for an appointment with Dr. Love when you called

19   Regency?

20

21   A.   I can't really remember. I may have just asked for an evaluation for cosmetic

22   surgery.

23

24   Q.   Would you have used the term "cosmetic," as opposed to "plastic," surgery?

25

26   A.   I could have used either. To me, they're the same.

1 No, I didn't know that Dr. Love was a dermatologist when I made that phone call. I didn't

2 learn that until I had my appointment at Regency. My appointment was scheduled for

3 about a week after I called. I filled out some paperwork and talked to a nurse, then

4 I talked to a doctor who explained the types of procedures that they could do. During that

5 conversation, I asked whether I would get to meet Dr. Love. The doctor I was talking to

6 told me that this was not Dr. Love's office. He said that Dr. Love was a dermatologist, not a

7 plastic surgeon, and that I'd be much better off with a fully qualified plastic surgeon. I felt

8 that this was sort of a hard sell, so I said I'd think about everything he told me, and I left.

9

10 I thought it was a hard sell because I was there to discuss facial procedures, and this guy

11 was telling me about liposuction, and body contouring, and tummy tucks. Way more than

12 I was interested in. Plus, he sounded pretty negative about Dr. Love. I thought that was

13 kind of unprofessional.

14

15 Within a couple of weeks I actually saw Dr. Love. I found his number online and made an

16 appointment, and I really liked him. No hard sell at all. He explained what he could do, and

17 how much it would cost. He showed me some before-and-after pictures, and told me to

18 think about it and discuss it with my husband, and let him know if I wanted to go ahead.

19 I decided to go forward and it went exactly as Dr. Love said it would.

20

21 Yes, Dr. Love did tell me that I would have the Love Look. As a matter of fact, he joked about

22 that. And to tell you the truth, both my husband and I love the look that resulted.

23

24 I don't recall whether, when I was at Regency's office, anyone mentioned the Love Look or

25 the Look of Love or anything like that.

26

27 Yes, I guess the bottom line is that I got exactly what you wanted from exactly the doctor

28 I wanted. But only after wasting two hours at Regency.

1 Yes, I've continued to treat with Dr. Love, as I've said, for Botox, and one of my boys has

2 seen him for acne. He and Mrs. Love hired my firm as their realtor when they sold their

3 house and bought a condo. He's also been very generous in supporting the annual Central

4 City Hospice fundraising auction. For each of the last three years, he's donated $1,000

5 worth of Botox injections. I'm president of the hospice board of trustees, and I recruited

6 Dr. Love's donations.

7

8 No, I've never socialized with Dr. or Mrs. Love except at the auction. They sit at our table.

9

10 No, Dr. Love didn't ask me to be a witness in this case. Actually, Mrs. Love did at the auction.

11 She told me that Regency has really screwed Dr. Love over, and I said I'd be happy to help

12 if I could.

13

14 I have read the foregoing, and it an accurate transcription of my deposition testimony

15 given on Feb. 20, YR-1.

Catherine Delp

Diana Segan
Jan. 12, YR-0

1 My name is Diana Segan, MD. I graduated from Cornell Medical School in YR-29, then

2 took a general surgery residency at Northwestern and a plastic surgery fellowship at the

3 University of Pennsylvania, which I completed in YR-21. I'm board certified in both general

4 surgery and plastics. I am an unpaid clinical associate professor at the Columbia University

5 School of Medicine. I don't teach formal classes, but I have plastic surgery fellows assigned

6 to thirty-day rotations in our New York City office.

7

8 I now practice only nine months a year. I take off three months, and devote one of those

9 months to medical missionary work in East Africa. The great majority of that work is

10 reconstructive surgery, about 60 percent with children and 40 percent with adults. The

11 sponsor is DOC, Doctors Operating for Christ.

12

13 I am a shareholder in Regency Plastic Surgery, PC. I was president of the corporation

14 from its founding in October YR-13 until October YR-3, when Dr. Dale Tremble, one of the

15 younger New York City surgeons, took over. We have sixteen shareholders, all of whom are

16 Regency surgeons. We also employ six non-shareholder surgeons and a number of nurses

17 and physician assistants, and of course clerical and business personnel.

18

19 After I completed my fellowship, I was hired by Grossman and Levine, a New York plastic

20 surgery partnership. Dr. Grossman and Dr. Levine were the partners, and Dr. Nathan

21 Yale and I were employees. We eventually became partners and took over the practice in

22 YR-13, when Drs. Grossman and Levine retired. We purchased their interests over ten

23 years. We incorporated as Regency Plastic Surgery, PC, with each of us owning 50 percent

24 of the stock.

1   Q.   What changes did you make after taking over the practice thirteen years ago?

2

3   A.   The old practice was traditional plastic surgery, with about 40 percent

4   reconstructive surgery, accident injuries, burns, and the like. The other was

5   60 percent elective cosmetic surgery. Nathan and I decided to transition as

6   quickly as possible to 100 percent cosmetic surgery.

7

8   Q.   Why?

9

10   A.   That would allow us to avoid the increasing hassles with insurance

11   companies and Medicare/Medicaid over coverage and charges for

12   reconstructive surgery. As a cosmetic-only practice, there's no insurance

13   involved. We're paid directly by our patients—cash or credit cards—or

14   by companies that specialize in financing cosmetic surgery.

15

16 Yes, we're paid 100 percent in advance. We have virtually no receivables.

17

18 Our vision for Regency has always been to enhance our patients' self-esteem and success

19 by improving their appearance. We believe that our patients lead more fulfilling lives both

20 personally and economically as a result of our treatment. That is based on the fact that so

21 many of our new patients are referrals from former patients.

22

23 One of the first things we did when we took over the old practice was to retain Urban

24 Contacts, a boutique marketing and advertising agency in New York. They came up with

25 the name Regency, which we liked because it symbolized the high quality that was our

26 aim for the practice. Urban recommended that we limit our marketing activities to print

27 media, rather than television, which they thought could cheapen our services. They said we

28 shouldn't compete for viewer attention with the hundreds of lawyers who are promising

29 to get money for people. In particular, Urban recommended that we advertise in what they

30 called "Gucci glossies." Those are slick, upscale magazines that are aimed at people with

1 significant disposable income and who are concerned with their image, the kind of people

2 who shop at Gucci.

3

4 Urban suggested a couple of marketing themes that we rejected as to cutesy. No, I can't recall

5 what they were. Then they hit on The Look of Love, which we really liked. At first we were

6 concerned that it might be illegal to use a song title for our slogan, but Urban assured us that

7 no one can own rights to a title. They focus-grouped the slogan in connection with cosmetic

8 surgery, and it got a good response, especially from upper-income people. So they built our

9 marketing campaign around the slogan. At first, it was limited to the Gucci glossies, but later,

10 like everyone, we expanded to the web. We also expanded to theater and concert programs.

11

12 Urban took care of registering The Look of Love with the U.S. Patent and Trademark Office

13 as our slogan.

14

15   Q.   Please look at Exhibit 5. Is that a letter you received from Urban relating to

16   registration.

17

18   A.   Yes.

19

20   Q.   And it specifically refers to Dr. Love?

21

22   A.   Yes, but I don't think I remembered it when we moved into the Central

23   City area.

24

25 Our marketing goal was to establish Regency as a provider of first-class cosmetic surgery

26 procedures. All our ads reference the kinds of procedures that we perform, and that all our

27 physicians are board-certified plastic surgeons who are also members of the American

28 College of Plastic Surgeons. Yes, our ads contain pictures of attractive people, but not

29 anything that is sexually suggestive. No, we never thought The Look of Love meant that

30 our patients would be more successful in their sex lives. Yes, we did mean to suggest that

1 our patients could be more successful in their love lives, as well as their professional lives

2 and their everyday lives. Yes, I suppose that sex can play a part in one's love live. No, of

3 course the pictures in our ads are not pictures of our former patients—that would be

4 unethical. The people in the pictures are models that Urban hires for photo shoots. I don't

5 think they've ever used stock photos, but I'm not 100 percent certain.

6

7 The campaign has been very effective. Our New York City practice expanded to four

8 surgeons within a couple of years, and in YR-10 we purchased practices in Stamford,

9 CT and Saddle River, NJ. We paid for those practices with cash over time and Regency

10 stock. In YR-8, we purchased practices in Buckhead, GA and Naples, FL. In each case, the

11 surgeons whose practices we purchased joined Regency, and in each case, the gross and

12 net incomes of the offices increased substantially. During the first year in each location,

13 we achieved about a 10 percent revenue increase. After the first year, the practices showed

14 annual revenue increases of 3 to 5 percent. We attribute the increases to increased patient

15 load per surgeon, increased efficiency in medical and business practices, our ability to

16 negotiate more favorable financial arrangements with the facilities at which we operate,

17 and greater selectivity in the procedures we perform. Yes, we believe The Look of Love

18 campaign is responsible, at least in part, for the increased patient loads, but how big a part

19 I can't say.

20

21 Yes, the numbers were even better in Oakdale than in our other satellite offices. We

22 increased revenues in Oakdale by 20 percent the first year and averaged about

23 8.5 percent in later years. We believe that Oakdale did better than our other offices

24 because, until recently, no other plastic surgery practice in the area engaged in any

25 significant marketing campaign.

26

27 Yes, we still use Urban Contacts for our advertising. They do the artwork, find the

28 appropriate media, and help us with web search utilization. For some years now, we've for

29 paid for an ad link on Google for searches that originate in the areas where we have offices,

30 and that use the terms "cosmetic" or "plastic" with the terms "surgery," "love," or "look."

1   The most frequent procedures that Regency surgeons perform are facelifts; eyelid surgery;

2   breast surgery including lifts, augmentation, and reduction; body contouring; liposuction;

3   tummy tucks; rhinoplasty; and injectables such as Botox and collagen. No, not every

4   Regency surgeon does each procedure, but each procedure is available at each of our

5   offices. Our surgeons do not do laser skin procedures, dermabrasion, spider or varicose

6   vein procedures, or small procedures like mole removals. We leave those to our physician

7   assistants or we refer patients to outside specialties, most often dermatology, because those

8   procedures don't require the training and experience of board-certified plastic surgeons.

9

10 In YR-6, we purchased Drs. Waters and Connelly's practice in Oakdale. Yes, it's a well-

11 to-do bedroom community outside of Central City. Drs. Waters and Connelly wanted to

12 slow down—they were both in their fifties—and they approached us about a possible

13 deal. I negotiated the deal with them myself. I reviewed their books and their patient

14 charts, inspected their office and the hospital where they operate, and talked to surgeons

15 who were familiar with their work. Our business people talked to their business people.

16 The whole due diligence process took about 120 days. We agreed to pay Drs. Waters and

17 Connelly $500,000 each over a five-year period.

18

19 Yes, the issue of Dr. Love's slogan was discussed during that time. They told me that Dr. Love

20 was a local dermatologist who had used a similar slogan in cheesy, cable TV commercials

21 for some years. They didn't know much about Dr. Love's practice, but were under the

22 impression that cosmetic procedures were a small part of his practice and were limited to

23 minor procedures like dermabrasion and mole removals. Dr. Connelly said that Dr. Love

24 and Regency couldn't be more different. "Like the Dress Barn and Saks Fifth Avenue" is

25 how I think he put it. Yes, I watched one of the commercials, which Dr. Connelly recorded

26 for me, and I agreed with his analysis. We briefly discussed asking Dr. Love to stop using

27 his non-registered slogan, but decided that it would be unwise for the new kid on the block

28 to make waves. No, it never crossed our minds that our use of our registered slogan might

29 violate Dr. Love's rights. No, our discussion about Dr. Love did not refresh my recollection

30 of having received Exhibit 5.

1 Yes, Exhibit 10 appears to be an email exchange between Bob Connelly and me, but

2 I don't specifically remember it. Yes, I understand you obtained it when you subpoenaed

3 Bob's records. No, we don't have a copy of it in Regency's records. We regularly purge all

4 nonpatient-related emails that are more than three years old. Yes, I visited Bob and Carl

5 in Oakdale in November, YR-5 as part of our due diligence. I have no reason to believe that

6 I didn't engage in that email exchange, but I just don't remember it.

7

8 Exhibit 11 is the website home page that we used for a couple of years. Urban designed

9 it for us and I approved it. No, the endorsements don't come from actual patients, nor do

10 the before and after pictures. We would never ask our patients to display themselves or

11 to make public statements about their surgery. I think the copywriters at Urban wrote the

12 endorsements and found the pictures somewhere. We reviewed them to make sure they

13 accurately reflected out patients' feelings and results. No, I never intended to capitalize

14 on Dr. Love's slogan in any way. I'm sure that I never even thought about Dr. Love or his

15 slogan when I approved the homepage. We stopped using the endorsement about "I love

16 the look" after Dr. Love filed suit. Yes, that was after our lawyers in this case looked at

17 the website.

18

19 When I got Dr. Love's letter of September 13, YR-6, I was very surprised because we had

20 registered our slogan and had been using it for six years without any problem. My first

21 instinct was to ignore the letter, but I sent it to Kal Foster at Urban. She discussed it with

22 their trademark lawyer and gave me most of the language I used in my response to Dr. Love.

23 Yes, Exhibit 6 is a copy of the letter I sent. No, I did not intend in my response to imply that

24 we were competing with him for cosmetic surgery patients, but not dermatology patients.

25 Based on what Dr. Waters had told me, I didn't think we were competing with him at all.

26 I intended simply to reassure Dr. Love that we weren't trying to take his patients away

27 from him.

28

29 I didn't hear from Dr. Love after my response, and I figured that he was comfortable that

30 Regency didn't pose any threat to this practice. So I was shocked when, out of the blue, he

1 sued us. Between the time I received his letter and the time he filed suit, we probably spent

2 about $120,000 in marketing our Look of Love campaign in the Central City area.

3

4 I believe Dr. Love's claims are frivolous. We do different procedures, we're engaged in

5 different specialties, and we advertise in different media. Yes, after Dr. Love filed suit I did

6 ask Dr. Waters whether he knew of any confusion between Regency and Dr. Love. He told

7 me that on maybe three or four occasions the Oakdale office received phone calls asking

8 for an appointment with Dr. Love. Of course, that is second- or third-hand information.

9 Dr. Waters told me that on those occasions the callers were given Dr. Love's phone number,

10 which our receptionist knew from his commercials: 1-800-LOVLOOK.

11

12 Yes, Regency's Oakdale office has been quite successful. Drs. Connelly and Waters are

13 still practicing full time, and as of the first of this year we added a third plastic surgeon.

14 Exhibit 7 is a summary of the Oakdale office financials since we opened it.

15

16 I know we have a Facebook page but I've never seen it. I'm not on Facebook and have

17 never used it. Kal Foster at Urban takes care of social media for us.

18

19 I have read the foregoing, and it an accurate transcription of my deposition testimony

20 given on Jan. 12, YR-0.

Diana Segan, MD

Jeffrey Anderson
Jan. 15, YR-0

1 I'm Jeffrey Anderson. I live at 4285 Forest Street, Central City. I'm forty-nine years old. I'm

2 a computer programmer with Atlas Engineering in Central City. I'm divorced. I have three

3 kids, two girls and a boy.

4

5 Yes, I've been a patient of Regency Plastic Surgery's Oakdale office. I had three liposuction

6 procedures there in YR-3. I'd been divorced for three years and I wasn't having much luck

7 with the dating process. I'd gained some weight in my forties and I thought that my weight

8 might be part of the problem. It seemed like liposuction would be the quickest way to

9 improve my appearance, so I consulted with Regency and then I had the procedures. Plus,

10 I started a diet and exercise program at a gym.

11

12 I decided on Regency because I'd seen their ads in Central City Monthly. I called to see if

13 they did liposuction. I made an appointment with Dr. Waters, who I really liked. I agreed to

14 his plan for three procedures. I've been extremely satisfied with the results.

15

16   Q.   What was it about Regency's ads that persuaded you to call them?

17

18   A.   They were professional and discreet.

19

20   Q.   Is Exhibit 8 one of the ads you saw?

21

22   A.   I can't say for sure, but that's the tone of the ads I saw.

23

24   Q.   Was the slogan "The Look of Love" a factor in your decision to call Regency?

25

26   A.   Not in and of itself. It was the ads in total.

1 Yes, before I called Regency, I had seen Dr. Stanley Love's television commercials many

2 times. It's hard to live in Central City and not see them. I thought his commercials were

3 pretty cheesy. I had no interest is seeing a doctor who promotes himself on TV like a car

4 dealer or an injury lawyer. I never considered calling him. No, I didn't know that Dr. Love

5 was a dermatologist. From his commercials, I assumed that he was a plastic surgeon

6 because I thought that's who does cosmetic surgery.

7

8 I never thought the Regency ads in Central City Monthly might be ads for Dr. Love. The

9 whole tone of Regency's ads was way above Dr. Love's commercials. There's just no

10 similarity at all. It never crossed my mind that "The Love Look" and "The Look of Love"

11 were similar slogans.

12

13 I know that's true for other Regency patients as well. After I had my procedures, I joined

14 a support group that Regency had formed so we could help each other with our efforts

15 to lose weight and keep it off. I went to meetings for about six months. More than once,

16 we joked about Dr. Love and his cheesy commercials. Everyone agreed that they would

17 never go to him for surgery. No one ever said they'd been confused between Dr. Love and

18 Regency. There were about twenty people in the group.

19

20 I know two people who have been treated by Dr. Love. My daughter, Amanda, went to him

21 about five years ago when she was thirteen for her acne. That was at the suggestion of her

22 aunt, my former wife's sister. I drove Amanda to her appointment and waited for her in

23 Dr. Love's waiting room. After about twenty minutes, she came back to the waiting room in

24 tears, all upset. All she could say was, "Let's get out of here." When we got outside, she told

25 me that Dr. Love was horrible to her, that he called her a spoiled brat. She calmed down

26 only when I promised her that she'd never have to see Dr. Love again.

27

28 Yes, my former sister-in-law is the other person I know who went to Dr. Love. She had

29 him remove the wrinkles around her eyes and mouth. She thought she looked wonderful.

30 I couldn't see any difference. I thought she was ugly before her surgery, and ugly after.

1 I admit I was never particularly fond of my sister-in-law. She had her surgery done a couple

2 of years before me and my wife split up. She's a clinical psychologist, just like my wife.

3

4 Yes, my wife has remarried. No, I haven't.

5

6 Yes, I've been convicted of a felony. I was convicted of embezzlement over $1,000 about

7 seven years ago. I was initially charged with embezzlement over $10,000 from the

8 computer consulting firm I worked for. I didn't embezzle any money; I just made a stupid

9 mistake in a $15,000 overpayment to a hardware contractor. The problem was that the

10 contractor was my old college roommate, and I made the overpayment about three weeks

11 before he loaned me $12,000 to pay off a gambling debt.

12

13 I pled guilty because my lawyer told me that my story, even though it was true, sounded

14 fishy, and I was facing a ten-year maximum sentence on the original charge. So she plea-

15 bargained a deal for me to plead to the lesser charge, which had an eighteen month max.

16 I told the judge that I was guilty, because my lawyer said it was the only way to get the plea

17 deal. I was sentenced to six months in the county jail, plus restitution. I was released after

18 four months because the jail was overcrowded. I made full restitution, even though it took

19 a while. I've not had any trouble with the law since then. I had trouble finding work after

20 that; it was hard because I had a felony conviction on my record, but I've had my present

21 job for about five years and it's going well.

22

23 I have read the foregoing, and it an accurate transcription of my deposition testimony

24 given on March 1, YR-1.

Jeffrey Anderson

Expert Materials

PLAINTIFFS' LIABILITY EXPERT'S MATERIALS

Medical Dynamics
The Marketing of Medicine

Pat Brantly, MD, MBA
President

Mr. Carl Schmidt
Schmidt, Warren & Rothschild
400 S. Ashley St.
Central City, Nita 80144

Dear Mr. Schmidt,

Thank you for sending this matter to me for evaluation.

You asked me to determine, from a medical marketing standpoint, whether potential cosmetic surgery patients are likely to be confused between Dr. Stanley Love's and Regency Plastic Surgery's marketing campaigns in the Central City, Nita, area.

To make that determination, I reviewed the depositions of Drs. Love and Segan and of Catherine Delp and Jeffrey Anderson; the financial records of Dr. Love's and Regency's Central City-area offices; representative samples of Dr. Love's television commercials and Regency's magazine advertisements; the parties' websites; and the survey that Survey Research Associates ("SRA") designed and performed at my request.

I base my opinion on those materials, and on my medical and marketing training. I have seventeen years of medical experience in private practice, as well as eight years of experience in consulting with other physicians and medical practices on marketing issues.

2700 First Bank Tower
Chicago, Illinois 60611
312.555.5304

In my opinion, there is more than just a high likelihood that Regency's "Look of Love" campaign might confuse patients; documented confusion has, in fact, occurred. Potential patients of Dr. Love have mistakenly called Regency's Central City-area office on a number of occasions. The only practical reason that a patient seeking an appointment with Dr. Love would call Regency is that "The Look of Love" campaign led the patient to conclude that if she called the phone number in "The Look of Love" ad, she would reach Dr. Stanley Love's office. This is confirmed by Ms. Delp's testimony and by Dr. Love's testimony about the woman he met at a charity function who told him that she mistakenly went to Regency instead of to Dr. Love. This woman's experience demonstrates the damage done to Dr. Love: despite intending to use his services, her misunderstanding resulted in her having her surgery at Regency.

We know about this one case only because the woman happened to run into Dr. Love and tell him about her experience. We cannot know how many other patients who intended to see Dr. Love wound up with appointments at Regency. In my estimation, there have probably been a substantial number, because these patients asked for an appointment for a specific concern, not a specific doctor. In my years of internal medicine practice in a seven-physician office, many patients asked to be seen for a specific concern, not to be seen by a specific physician. Thus, if a patient intending to call Dr. Love's office mistakenly called Regency and asked for a facelift evaluation, the patient would wind up with an appointment at Regency. Indeed, Ms. Delp continued to believe that Regency was an office of Dr. Love's even during the first part of her appointment, and the caller who first alerted Dr. Love to Regency's campaign assumed that the Oakdale office was associated with Dr. Love. Other patients of Regency could easily have come in—and even remained throughout treatment—having decided to stick with Regency doctors.

My opinion is supported by the survey performed by SRA. SRA designed the survey to test the likelihood of confusion between Dr. Love's "The Love Look" campaign and Regency's "The Look of Love" campaign. I instructed SRA to limit the survey to ages twenty-five to sixty-five because I found on the American Society of Cosmetic Surgeons website that almost 90 percent of cosmetic surgery patients fall into that age range.

The survey shows that there is a high likelihood of confusion, as Question Five makes abundantly clear. Moreover, Question Four reflects the actual confusion that both Dr. Love and Dr. Segan discussed in their depositions. If 25 to 42 percent of potential patients assume that "The Look of Love" advertisement is for Dr. Love and call the Regency office based on that misassumption, the loss of patients and revenue for Dr. Love is inevitable.

The question arises why Dr. Love is not able to identify more patients who made this error. But it is not surprising that we do not know the identity of any patients who mistakenly went to Regency and actually had surgery there. The identity of those patients is protected by law, including HIPAA, and by medical ethics.

Over the course of my years at Medical Dynamics, I have provided marketing consultation to more than 300 medical and dental providers in the Midwest, ranging from sole practitioners to groups as large as twenty. I have become all too familiar with the pernicious practices of multistate medical corporations such as Regency. Their principle goal is to grow themselves by taking patients away from long-serving, local providers, much the same way that "big box" stores have taken business from local merchants.

One of the most effective weapons in the multistate medical corporation's arsenal is the slick advertising campaign. That was certainly Regency's tactic in the Central City area. Even in the face of Dr. Love's early protest, Regency persisted in its infringing campaign. They even purchased a Google ad that would top the list if anyone searched for cosmetic surgery and "The Love Look." There is no question in my mind that Regency's infringement was "willful," as you have explained the legal definition of that term.

I will be pleased to testify in this matter. My fee, as I believe you know, is $700 per hour for all activity devoted to this case.

Very truly yours,

P. Brantly

Pat Brantly, MD, MBA

Survey Research Associates
Chicago, IL

Mail Survey Conducted for Medical Dynamics
345 Nita City-Area Residents (response rate: 64%)
Age Range: 25–65

1. Have you seen Dr. Stanley Love's television commercials in which he talks about "The Love Look"?

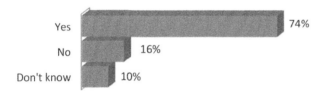

Yes — 74%
No — 16%
Don't know — 10%

If your answer is "yes" answer Questions 2 and 3. If your answer is "no" go to Question #5.

2. Do you believe "The Love Look" refers to Dr. Love's cosmetic surgical results:

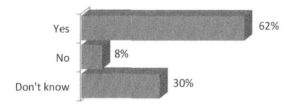

Yes — 62%
No — 8%
Don't know — 30%

3. Have you also seen magazine ads for cosmetic surgery in which the phrase "The Look of Love" was featured?

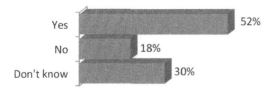

Yes — 52%
No — 18%
Don't know — 30%

If your answer is "yes" answer Question 4. If your answer is "no" go to Question #5.

4. When you saw the magazine ads, did you believe "The Look of Love" referred to Dr. Stanley Love's cosmetic surgery?

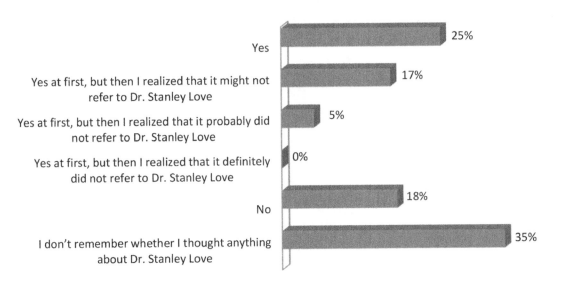

Yes — 25%

Yes at first, but then I realized that it might not refer to Dr. Stanley Love — 17%

Yes at first, but then I realized that it probably did not refer to Dr. Stanley Love — 5%

Yes at first, but then I realized that it definitely did not refer to Dr. Stanley Love — 0%

No — 18%

I don't remember whether I thought anything about Dr. Stanley Love — 35%

5. With reference to cosmetic surgery, do you believe the phrases "The Love Look" and "The Look of Love" are:

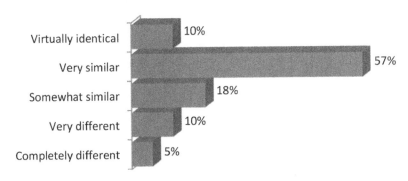

Virtually identical — 10%

Very similar — 57%

Somewhat similar — 18%

Very different — 10%

Completely different — 5%

6. List the name(s) of any doctor(s) you assume are associated with the medical corporation entitled "Stanley Love, M D, PC":

Dr. Stanley Love — 98%

No idea — 2%

7. List the name(s) of any doctor(s) you assume are associated with the medical corporation entitled "Regency Plastic Surgery, P C":

Dr. Stanley Love — 98%

No idea — 2%

Pat Brantly, MD, MBA

Current Position

President, Medical Dynamics, Chicago, IL

Professional Employment

YR-17 to date	Practicing physician, Partners in Internal Medicine, Lake Forest, IL
YR-7 to date	Medical marketing consultant, Medical Dynamics

Education

YR-25	BA, Miami University of Ohio
YR-21	MD, Wight State University
YRS-21–YR-18	Internal Medicine Residency, Detroit Medical Center (Wayne State Univ.)
YR-8	MBA, University of Phoenix

Professional Organizations

Illinois State Medical Society

Lake County Medical Association

American Medical Association

Member, American Association of Medical Executives

Founding Member, American Society of Medical Marketing Consultants

Publications

Eight articles on medical marketing

Expert Witness Retention

Retained in fourteen cases, all of behalf of plaintiff

Honors

Listed in Chicagoland Magazine's *Compilation of Best Docs*

Outstanding Resident Award, Detroit Medical Center, YR-17

Community Service Award, Chicagoland chapter of ACLU, YR-4

Person of the Year, Chicagoland Toastmasters Club, YR-3

Certification

American Board of Internal Medicine

DEFENDANT'S LIABILITY EXPERT'S MATERIALS

Jean Woodward, PhD
4478 Silver Lake Rd.
Edina, MN

Ms. Alicia Robertson
Kilpatrick, Stone & Shah
1400 Vernor Ave.
Central City, Nita 80144

Dear Ms. Robertson,

You asked me to determine the likelihood of confusion between Dr. Stanley Love's "The Love Look" marketing campaign and Regency Plastic Surgery, PC's "The Look of Love"® marketing campaign. To that end, I have reviewed Dr. Love's and Dr. Segan's depositions and the Delp and Anderson depositions. I have also researched the field of cosmetic surgery, analyzed the two marketing campaigns, and conducted a survey and focus group.

My survey was conducted by mail of Central City-area people aged forty to seventy years. I chose that age range because my research revealed that it is the most common for cosmetic surgery. Potential participants were randomly selected from area telephone directories. They were contacted by telephone to determine whether they were within the targeted age range, and whether they were willing to participate in a "consumer survey." We did not identify the nature of the survey. We assured each potential participant that we were not attempting to sell anything, and that their identities would not be revealed or provided to anyone. We sent the questionnaire to the 338 persons who agreed to participate, and received 264 completed questionnaires.

My analysis revealed that, although the campaigns' themes may seem similar at first glance, they are actually quite different. "The Love Look" is a phrase that is not in common parlance. Rather, it describes something that is unique to Dr. Love, either by identifying him as the doctor who performs certain surgeries, or simply as an advertising slogan that makes clever use of his name.

"The Look of Love"®, on the other hand, is a phrase that is in common parlance, principally because it is the title of a popular song that has been recorded by several well-known artists, including Dusty Springfield and Diana Krall. The phrase, largely as a result of the song's lyrics, denotes a look that conveys the emotion of love. It does not identify, directly or indirectly, a doctor who has performed surgery. The phrase, when applied to plastic surgery, is quite fanciful and quite different from "The Love Look."

"The Look of Love"® campaign makes it clear that Regency's doctors are plastic surgeons. By contrast, as my survey demonstrates, less than half the people familiar with Dr. Love's commercials believe that he is a plastic surgeon. Thus, there is a greater likelihood of distinction, as opposed to confusion, relating to the sources of the parties' services.

Anecdotally, a small number of patients have mistakenly called Regency's Oakdale office in an attempt to reach Dr. Love. Because this insignificant number of mistaken potential patients had their temporary misunderstanding immediately resolved when they were given Dr. Love's phone number, there was no resultant loss of business to Dr. Love. My survey reveals that there is virtually no chance that such a mistake would result in someone making an appointment with a Regency plastic surgeon rather than Dr. Love, let alone having surgery performed by a Regency surgeon rather than Dr. Love.

The parties, in the main, use different marketing channels. Regency uses print media aimed at a specific demographic (well-to-do adults), while Dr. Love uses cable television channels, which reach a much wider demographic. Although there may be some overlap, I believe it is not significant.

Finally, and importantly, I presented two fifty-person focus groups (with the same demographics as the survey group) with side-by-side comparisons of one of Dr. Love's commercials and one of Regency's magazine's ads. Both were representative of their overall campaigns. For one group, I presented Dr. Love's commercial first, then presented an enlarged copy of a Regency ad. For the other, I reversed the order. I then provided the following questionnaire to the group members.

> — I believe the commercial and the ad are for the same doctors.

> — I believe the commercial and the ad are for different doctors.

> — I can't tell whether the commercial and the ad are for the same or different doctors.

There was no statistically significant difference in the results between the two groups. In the first group, two people chose the first option, forty-four people chose the second, and four chose the third. In the second group, one person chose the first option, forty-eight people chose the second, and one chose the third. My conclusion is that this demonstrated an extremely low (verging on nonexistent) likelihood of confusion.

Based on the above, I conclude that there is an extremely low likelihood of confusion between Dr. Love's and Regency's campaigns. Therefore, I conclude that Regency has not impinged on any common law trademark that Dr. Love might hold.

I will be pleased to testify in accordance with my opinions. My fee schedule is as follows:

> Review of materials: $400 per hour

> Survey research: $500 per hour

Deposition testimony: $700 per hour (four-hour minimum)

Trial testimony: $7,000 per day (one-day minimum)

Travel: $350 per hour plus expenses (including business-class plane fare)

Please call with any questions.

Yours truly,

Jean Woodward

Jean Woodward, PhD

Central City Cosmetic Advertisement Survey
Conducted by Phyllis Woodward, PhD

1 Have you seen Dr. Stanley Love's television commercials in which he uses the phrase, "The Love Look"?

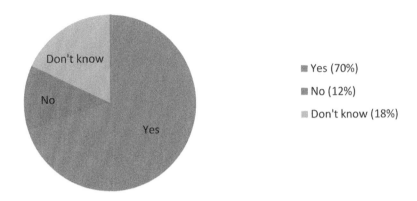

- Yes (70%)
- No (12%)
- Don't know (18%)

If your answer is "yes", answer Questions 2, and 3.
If your answer is "no" or "don't know", go to Question #4.

2 Do you believe "The Love Look" refers to:

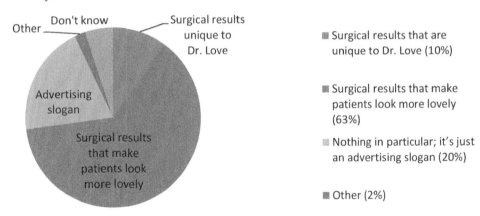

- Surgical results that are unique to Dr. Love (10%)
- Surgical results that make patients look more lovely (63%)
- Nothing in particular; it's just an advertising slogan (20%)
- Other (2%)

3 Do you believe that Dr. Stanley Love is a:

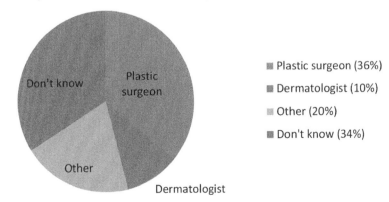

- Plastic surgeon (36%)
- Dermatologist (10%)
- Other (20%)
- Don't know (34%)

4 Who do you think have more extensive training and experience in cosmetic surgery:

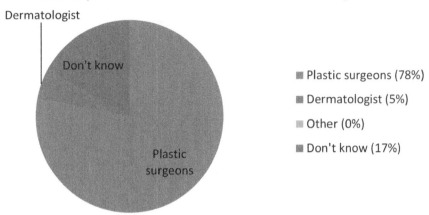

Dermatologist

Don't know

Plastic
surgeons

■ Plastic surgeons (78%)

■ Dermatologist (5%)

■ Other (0%)

■ Don't know (17%)

5 Have you seen Regency Plastic Surgery's magazine advertisements?

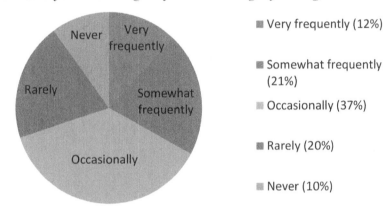

Never Very
frequently

Rarely

Somewhat
frequently

Occasionally

■ Very frequently (12%)

■ Somewhat frequently
(21%)

■ Occasionally (37%)

■ Rarely (20%)

■ Never (10%)

6 Do you believe that the doctors at Regency Plastic Surgery are most likely:

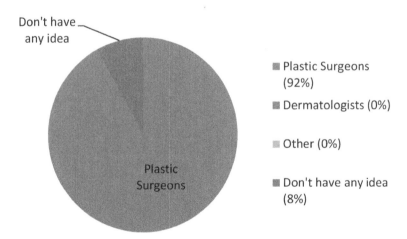

Don't have
any idea

Plastic
Surgeons

■ Plastic Surgeons
(92%)

■ Dermatologists (0%)

■ Other (0%)

■ Don't have any idea
(8%)

7 If you intended to schedule an appointment with a specific doctor, but mistakenly called the wrong doctor's office, would you:

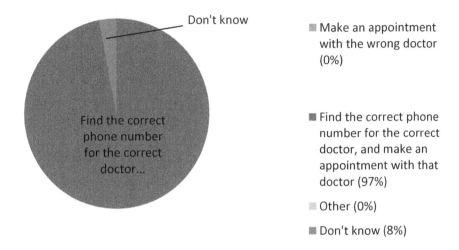

Don't know

Find the correct phone number for the correct doctor...

- Make an appointment with the wrong doctor (0%)

- Find the correct phone number for the correct doctor, and make an appointment with that doctor (97%)

- Other (0%)

- Don't know (8%)

8 Have you, or an immediate family member, ever had cosmetic surgery performed?

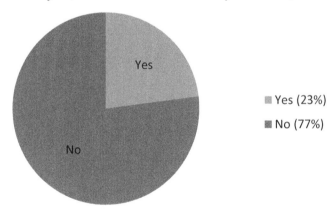

Yes

No

- Yes (23%)
- No (77%)

If your answer is "yes" answer Question 9. If your answer is "no" there are no further questions.

9 Who performed the surgery?

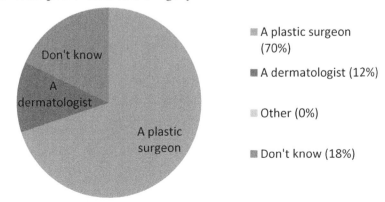

Don't know

A dermatologist

A plastic surgeon

- A plastic surgeon (70%)

- A dermatologist (12%)

- Other (0%)

- Don't know (18%)

Jean Woodward, PhD

4478 Silver Lake Road

Edina, MN

CURRENT POSITION

Rosenfire Professor of Marketing, Chair of Department of Marketing, University of Minnesota School of Management

EDUCATION

BA, Stanford University

MBA, University of Chicago

PhD in behavioral psychology, University of Chicago

PROFESSIONAL EMPLOYMENT

Assistant Professor, Northern Illinois University

Associate Professor, University of Minnesota

Full Professor, University of Minnesota

Corporate consultation: Representative clients listed on Exhibit A

PROFESSIONAL ORGANIZATIONS

Editorial Review Board, American Journal of Marketing

Frequent reviewer, Journal of Consumer Research

Past-president, American Society of Consumer Marketing

Board of Directors, International Marketing Society

PUBLICATIONS

Thirty-nine articles on consumer marketing in peer reviewed journals

Two chapters in marketing textbooks

Chief editor, *Principles of Modern Marketing*

EXPERT WITNESS RETENTION

More than fifty cases, approximately 20 percent plaintiff, 80 percent defens

HONORS

Lifetime Achievement Award, American Society of Consumer Marketing

Outstanding Teacher Award, University of Minnesota School of Management

Community Service Award, Minnesota Boys' and Girls' Clubs

Voice of Reason Award, Minnesota Right to Life

Woodward CV Exhibit A

General Motors, Pontiac Division

CompUSA

Wendy's

Countrywide Mortgage

Minnesota Bar Association

American Academy of Plastic Surgeons

Circuit City

PepsiCo

NASCAR

Twin Cities Metro Transit Authority

Northwest Airlines

Allstate Insurance

America Online

Comcast

Altria

Borders Books

PLAINTIFFS' DAMAGES EXPERT'S MATERIALS

Forrester & Associates
Accounting and Bookkeeping Services
4220 Washington St.
Central City, Nita 80144

Mr. Carl Schmidt
Schmidt, Warren & Rothschild
400 S. Ashley St.
Central City, Nita 80144

Dear Mr. Schmidt,

As you know, I have served as Dr. Love's accountant for more than fifteen years. I am quite familiar with his personal and professional financial records, and have reviewed his and Dr. Segan's depositions, as well as Exhibits 4 and 7. As a resident of Central City, I am familiar with Dr. Love's television commercials. As a subscriber to Central City Monthly and the Central City Playhouse Broadway Revisited Series, I am also familiar with Regency's Look of Love ads.

There is no question in my mind that Regency's ad campaign has adversely affected Dr. Love's cosmetic surgery revenues. This did not occur because Regency created new competition with Dr. Love. Regency merely replaced an existing competitor's corporate structure; the actual competitors (the doctors) remained the same. Thus, the only thing that can account for the dramatic increase in Regency's cosmetic surgery business is its advertising campaign.

I believe that it took several years for Dr. Love to fully feel the effects of Regency's campaign. The small increase in his cosmetic surgery revenues in YR-6 is explained by the fact that many of his patients in that year were completing a series of procedures that they had agreed to before Regency started advertising in this area. Also, I know from conversations with Dr. Love that he frequently advises patients who have decided to have cosmetic surgery, but who do not have the money to pay for it, to contribute to a fund over time in order to accumulate the necessary sums. This is like a Christmas Club savings account. It often takes two or three years to accumulate the necessary sums. Thus, many of Dr. Love's YR-6 patients had decided to have Dr. Love perform their surgery before Regency started its campaign.

As a result of these financial factors, the impact of Regency's Look of Love campaign was not seen directly in Dr. Love's revenues until YR-5 when, for the first time, his cosmetic surgery revenues fell. The fact that his cosmetic surgery revenues have continued falling since YR-5, while his non-cosmetic revenues have increased, supports my conclusions.

From YR-10 through YR-7, Dr. Love's cosmetic surgery revenues increased at an average rate of 11 percent. If we conservatively assume that, absent Regency's Look of Love campaign, Dr. Love's revenues would have continued at half that rate increase (5.5 percent) through YR-1, his yearly projected revenues, and the losses when compared to his actual revenues are as follows:

Year	Projected	Actual	Loss
YR-6	342,348	326,100	16,248
YR-5	361,117	313,700	47,417
YR-4	380,978	293,200	87,778
YR-3	401,932	279,700	122,232
YR-2	424,038	270,500	153,538
YR-1	447,360	250,400	196,960

Dr. Love's cumulative losses for these six years amount to $624,173. The average annual loss is $104,029. When that average loss is extended through the remaining eleven years of Dr. Love's work life to age sixty-five, the total future losses are $1,144,319 (11 x $104,029). I have not adjusted for probable inflation, nor have I reduced these losses to present value. My assumption is that these adjustments would largely cancel each other out. Thus, the total past and future damages resulting from Regency's Look of Love campaign amount to $1,768,492.

An alternative measure of past damages is the amount Regency has profited by its infringement of Dr. Love's trademark. To make this computation, I used the revenue percentages by which Regency's Oakdale office exceeded the average of its other satellite offices, and applied the differences to Regency's gross profits in Oakdale. For YR-6, Oakdale exceeded the other Regency offices by 10 percent, which, applied to Oakdale's gross profits, is $64,061. For subsequent years, I have compared Oakdale's revenue increases to the average for the other offices (4 percent) as follows:

YEAR	GROSS PROFIT	% APPLIED	DAMAGES
YR-5	$756,293	10.25%	$77,520
YR-4	$1,002,161	9.55%	$95,706
YR-3	$1,102,081	2.8%	$30,858
YR-2	$1,127,683	.9%	$10,149
YR-1	$993,007	none	none

The total damages with this computation are the sum of the damages from YR-6 through YR-2: $278,394.

I have made both sets of computations in accordance with generally accepted accounting principles.

Although I have never before testified as an expert witness, I will be pleased to support Dr. Love's case. My fees are my standard accounting fees, $300 per hour.

Yours truly,

Sammi Forrester

Sammi Forrester, CPA

Sammi Forrester

4220 Washington St., Central City, Nita ♦ (330) 555-3827 ♦ sforrester@forrester3827.nita

Education

Central City State College, BA in accounting, YR-20

Employment

Edwards & Greer

Accountant, YR-20–YR-16

CPA, YR-16–YR-10

Forrester & Associates, CPA, YR-10 to date

Civic Activity

Central City Rotary Club, YR-20 to date

Central City Lions Club, YR-20 to date

Central City Chamber of Commerce, YR-20 to date

Central City Playhouse, Board of Trustees, YR-8–YR-4

Boy Scouts' Brave Heart Trail Counsel

Advisory Board, YR-10–YR-5

Eagle Scout candidate mentor, YR-14 to date

Lawton School PTA

Executive Board, YR-12–YR-8

President, YR-10–YR-9

Central City State College Alumni Association, Trustee, YR-6–YR-2

Central City Men's Choir, YR-12 to date

American Muslim Society, Central City Branch

Board Member, YR- 7–YR-1

President, YR-2

Central City United Way, Executive Board, YR-7–YR-3

Central City Food Bank, Advisory Board, YR-3 to date

Educational Activity

Teacher, Basic Bookkeeping, Central City Community College, YR-5 to date

Saturday School Teacher, Central City Mosque, YR-18 to date

Defendant's Damages Expert's Materials

Skyline Partners
Business Is Our Business
340 E. 63rd Street
New York, New York

Aaron Weinberg, CPA, JD

Ms. Alicia Robertson
Kilpatrick, Stone & Shah
1400 Vernor Ave.
Central City, Nita 80144

Dear Ms. Robertson,

I have reviewed the depositions of Drs. Love and Segan and the financial data contained in Exhibits 4 and 7. I have also researched the impact of new marketing campaigns on preexisting competitors, and the impact over time of vanity television commercials. Based upon my review and research, and my years as a CPA and business consultant, I have reached the conclusion that Regency's The Look of Love® campaign in the Central City area did not adversely impact Dr. Love's cosmetic surgery revenues.

Regency began marketing in the Central City area when it opened its Oakdale office in January YR-6. The marketing campaign focused on Regency's The Look of Love® slogan. It consists of ads in high-end magazines such as *Central City Monthly* and *Hour Central City*, and in programs for the Central City Playhouse and Central City Symphony.

Over the first two years of the campaign, Regency experienced an increase in revenues compared to the predecessor medical office. Because the surgeons were the same, I attribute the increase, at least in significant part, to the campaign. Importantly, there was also a significant increase in Dr. Love's cosmetic surgery revenues during those two years compared to earlier years. Thus, there is nothing to suggest that Regency's campaign resulted in any damage to Dr. Love. To the contrary, my research has demonstrated that, when a new player enters a market, there is frequently an industry-wide increase in revenue. This is an example of a rising tide lifting all boats.

Here, the relevant industry is cosmetic surgery in the Central City area. I believe that Regency's campaign increased public awareness of the benefits of cosmetic surgery and resulted in increased calls to all cosmetic surgery providers, including Dr. Love. Moreover, if there was any confusion in the public's mind between The Look of Love® and The Love Look, the confusion may just as well have resulted in people calling Dr. Love's office in response to Regency's campaign.

In YR-5, Dr. Love's cosmetic surgery revenues (but, after YR-4, not his non-cosmetic revenues) began to decline. The decline has continued to date. I believe the cause of the decline is that Dr. Love's commercials became stale and far less effective. My research (printout from Advertising Today Online attached) has demonstrated that so-called vanity television commercials (where a business owner or service provider is featured in the commercials) are usually effective for three to five years, but much less effective afterward. In essence, the personality becomes stale. This is especially true where, as in Dr. Love's case, the character of the commercials remains unchanged.

Thus, I believe that Dr. Love has suffered no damage as the result of Regency's The Look of Love® campaign. I will be happy to testify on Regency's behalf. My fees are $750 per hour for research/analysis/preparation, and $850 per hour for deposition and trial testimony.

Yours truly,

Aaron Weinberg

Aaron Weinberg, CPA, JD

Vanity Commercials' Limited Lives—
New Research Findings

by Olivia Lynch, staff writer

For her MBA thesis at Emory University's Goizueta Business School, Courtney Levinson, twenty-four, spent hour after hour watching so-called "vanity commercials." These commercials feature the very people whose products or services were being advertised. Ms. Levinson studied the commercials of car dealers, injury lawyers, replacement-window manufacturers, dentists, tax preparers, furniture sellers and for-profit college presidents in the Atlanta, GA area. She also interviewed twenty-two people who were in the commercials or representatives of their companies. Promised anonymity, these people discussed, in general terms, their revenue histories.

Of the twenty-two campaigns, twenty resulted in significant (5 to 12 percent) revenue growth during the first three years of the campaign. The other two resulted in little or no growth and were discontinued within that three-year period.

Looking at the twenty campaigns that showed significant growth, Ms. Levinson found that seven continued to show good growth (more than 3 percent) after the initial three-year period. The other thirteen showed less than 3 percent growth or no continued growth at all.

Without exception, the campaigns with good growth made changes in the character of their commercials over the years (look, message, or both). The other thirteen campaigns remained largely unchanged for the period of Ms. Levinson's study.

Based on these results, Ms. Levinson concluded that vanity commercials have a limited useful life, after which they provide no additional revenue. She found that to remain effective beyond three years, the character of such commercials must be changed.

I confirmed Ms. Levinson's findings by interviewing two prominent political consultants. They agreed that, from one political campaign to the next—even if separated by only two years—a candidate's commercial message must be changed.

Ms. Levinson will be submitting her thesis to marketing journals after she receives her degree. In the meantime, her advice to vanity advertisers is, "Keep it fresh."

Contact us

Subscribers

Archive

Guidelines

Privacy

Leave your feedback

Aaron Weinberg

Accountant

EDUCATION

- ❖ BA in accounting, University of Texas, YR-20

- ❖ MBA, Wharton School of Business, YR-18

- ❖ JD, New York Law School, YR-8

EMPLOYMENT

- ❖ Goldman, Sachs, New York City, YR-18–YR-15

- ❖ Skyline Partners, New York City

  - ➢ Accounting Associate, YR-15–YR-12

  - ➢ Accounting Partner, YR-12–YR-8

  - ➢ Litigation Support Partner, YR-8 to date

    Testified in deposition or trial on damage issues in more than 100 cases involving business disputes

Skyline Partners provides business and litigation support services through its eight domestic and three international offices. Skyline employs over 300 business, accounting, and legal professionals.

LICENSES

- ❖ CPA, YR-18 to date

- ❖ State Bar of New York, YR-7 to date

COMMUNITY SERVICE

- ❖ Advisory Board Member, New York City Marathon, YR-14–YR-8

- ❖ Board Member, New York City Chamber of Commerce, YR-12–YR-9

❖ Board Member, The Ronald Reagan Society, YR-10–YR-6

❖ Member, New York City Firefighters Pension Board, YR-6 to date

❖ Congregation Beth Shalom, New York City

> ➢ Board Member, YR-4 to date

> ➢ President, YR-2 to date

EDUCATIONAL ACTIVITIES

❖ Adjunct Professor of Accounting, City College of New York, YR-8 to date

❖ Frequent lecturer, School for Persuasive Expert Witnesses, YR-4 to date

EXHIBITS

Electronic copies of all exhibits, and the accompanying PowerPoint
presentation, can be found at the following website:
http://bit.ly/1P20Jea
Password: Love2

Exhibit 1

Dr. Stanley Love television commercial

Commercial can be viewed at the following website:

http://bit.ly/1P20Jea
Password: Love2

Exhibit 2

"The Love Look"

Cosmetic Procedures Available
in Our Office:

- Eyelid surgery
- Lip Augmentation
- Dermabrasion
- Collagen and other filler injections
- Botox
- Spider vein therapy
- Skin resurfacing
- Chemical peels
- Liposuction
- Laser treatments

Dr. Stanley Love, is a board certified
dermatologist, and a Fellow of
the American Academy of
Cosmetic Surgery.

What is the American Academy of Cosmetic
Surgery?

The American Academy of Cosmetic Surgery is
a professional medical society whose members
are dedicated to patient safety and physician
education in cosmetic surgery.

"How to find us"

Dr. Stanley Love, M.D., P.C.
Dermatology and Cosmetic Surgery
"The Love Look"
3345 Richton
Central City, Nita

Hours by Appointment
1-800-LOVLOOK
(1-800-568-5665)

"Cosmetic Surgery -
you owe it to yourself."

NOTE: Color copies of all exhibits can be found
at the following website:
http://bit.ly/1P20Jea
Password: Love2

"Cosmetic Surgery—You owe it to yourself."

You will feel at home in our
ultra-modern facilities:

Our most popular
cosmetic procedure...
Eyelid Surgery

Before...

...and after!

Our Staff:

Office Manager Bobbi

Nurse Debby

Stanley Love, M.D., P.C.
Dermatology and Cosmetic
Surgery
"The Love Look"
3345 Richton
Central City, Nita
1-800-568-5665

Exhibit 3

Stanley Love, MD, PC
Dermatology and Cosmetic Surgery—The Love Look
3345 Richton Ave.
Central City, Nita 80144

Sept. 13, YR–6

Diana Segan, MD
Regency Plastic Surgery
341 E. 66th Street
New York, NY 10065

Dear Dr. Segan,

For many years, I have successfully practiced dermatology and cosmetic surgery in Central City. Since YR–14, I have used "The Love Look" to promote the cosmetic surgery part of my practice. I am associated with the slogan and the slogan is associated with me.

I have invested many thousands of dollars in this promotion. I believe that Regency's use of my name and an almost identical slogan capitalizes on my investment and reputation, and constitutes an unfair and unethical business practice. I respectfully insist that you cease and desist.

I am relying on you to do the right thing.

Yours truly,

Stanley Love

Stanley Love, MD

Exhibit 4

Revenue Report for Dr. Stanley Love, MD PC

Medisoft Report Generator - Stanley Love, MD PC

Revenue Summary Cosmetic	Yr - 8	Yr - 7	Yr - 6	Yr - 5	Yr - 4	Yr - 3	Yr - 2	Yr - 1
Bleph Lower	26,600	36,100	30,700	28,400	26,000	24,000	23,200	24,000
Bleph Upper	36,100	47,500	40,200	38,000	33,000	29,900	26,700	25,500
Bleph Both	0	16,000	18,800	20,200	19,800	18,100	18,900	17,000
Botox	22,800	28,200	26,000	23,400	25,800	20,300	19,600	17,500
ChemPeel	17,600	10,800	13,800	18,400	15,400	16,800	22,000	20,800
Drmabras	15,000	22,500	20,500	21,600	23,100	23,400	21,500	22,200
Filler Inj	13,200	15,000	19,600	18,500	14,000	17,900	13,400	12,000
Laser Resrf Face	13,500	31,500	33,000	29,500	24,600	31,800	26,700	24,400
Lipo x1	60,800	70,400	65,100	63,500	61,500	50,400	49,900	44,100
Lipo x2	11,400	28,500	30,200	28,100	26,200	18,600	17,700	14,900
Lipo x3	0	2,800	6,200	6,500	5,200	6,200	6,500	6,400
Spider Vein Laser	17,600	15,200	22,000	17,600	18,600	22,300	24,400	21,600
Total Cosmetic	**292,600**	**324,500**	**326,100**	**313,700**	**293,200**	**279,700**	**270,500**	**250,400**
Total Non-cosmetic	365,200	377,900	362,000	344,400	344,600	368,900	377,300	378,100
Total Revenue	**657,800**	**702,400**	**688,100**	**658,100**	**637,800**	**648,600**	**647,800**	**628,500**
Expense Category								
Rent	88,000	88,000	92,000	92,000	100,000	100,000	108,000	108,000
Salaries & benefits	190,000	194,600	205,250	178,000	133,900	137,800	138,000	140,000
Advertising	54,000	55,000	57,500	54,600	52,700	55,200	48,600	53,500
Office Admin	57,524	65,214	80,546	82,157	84,600	98,450	98,800	94,320
Dr. Love salary	175,000	240,000	205,000	190,000	170,000	170,000	175,000	165,000
Medical Supplies	32,845	38,954	46,925	72,654	94,714	74,561	69,417	70,417
Total Expenses	**597,369**	**681,768**	**687,221**	**669,411**	**635,914**	**636,011**	**637,817**	**631,237**

Exhibit 5

Urban
Contacts

430 Broadway
New York, NY 10012
212.555.4747

May 6, YR-13

BY MESSENGER

Diana Segan, MD
Regency Plastic Surgery, PC
341 E. 66th Street
New York, NY

Dear Diana:

Hope you are well. We've completed our research on "The Look of Love" and I'm pleased to report that there are no significant conflicts out there. Other than a couple of clothing and makeup lines, a wedding planner, and an online dating service, there are only two issues that could even remotely be deemed as significant:

    1. A sex columnist in the S.F. Bay area calls herself the "Love Doctor." Her column in the *East Bay Express* is called "The Look of Love." The *East Bay Express* is a free newspaper with a limited local circulation, primarily appealing to gay, lesbian, and transsexual readers. This has no bearing for us.

    2. A dermatologist, Dr. Stanley Love in Central City, Nita, uses the term "The Love Look" to describe his practice in local newspaper advertising. "The Love Look" is not registered with the state or the feds. Dr. Love has not trademarked his slogan. He is not a plastic surgeon, and his practice is geographically remote from Regency's. Our trademark counsel has therefore assured us that his use of a similar phrase will not prevent our registering "The Look of Love" with the U.S. Patent and Trademark Office.

Based on this research, we will move forward to register "The Look of Love" with the U.S. Patent and Trademark Office as Regency's service mark. This registration means that Regency will have the exclusive, nationwide right to this slogan for cosmetic plastic surgery services. Registration should be complete within sixty days. Once that occurs, please make sure that Regency always displays the ® symbol with its use of the slogan.

We feel confident we can now proceed with "The Look of Love" campaign. I've enclosed three ad mockups for you to consider. We'll need your go-ahead within the week if we are to adhere to the schedule.

By the way, I have a new restaurant for you to try. Rome Commune—it's in the West Village and quite good. Maybe I'll take you for lunch to celebrate the kickoff of "The Look of Love"!

Talk to you soon.

Sincerely,

Kal Foster

Kal Foster
Account Supervisor

Exhibit 6

Regency Plastic Surgery, PC

October 6, YR-6

Stanley Love, MD, PC
Dermatologist
3345 Richton
Central City, Nita 80144

My Dear Dr. Love,

I received your letter of Sept. 13 with surprise, because we have never used "The Love Look" in our marketing. Rather, we have used The Look of Love®, which has been Regency Plastic Surgery, PC's registered service mark for more than six years. A simple check with the United States Patent and Trademark Office would have revealed that to you.

Regency has expended substantial resources in marketing "The Look of Love®" concept in the Central City area and elsewhere. We believe it is symbolic of the services we provide to our patients. We intend to continue our marketing campaign.

You may rest assured that we have no intention of using your slogan or extending our campaign to television, which, I am told, is your medium of choice. We will not compete with you for airtime, or for your dermatology patients.

I wish you continued success in your dermatology practice.

Yours,

Diana Segan

Diana Segan, MD

341 E. 66th Street New York, NY 202.555.3811

Exhibit 7

Revenue Report for Regency Plastic Surgery, PC

Regency Plastic Surgery
Yearly Procedure Productivity 2003-2008
Office 6 (Oakdale)

Procedure Revenue	Yr - 6	Yr - 5	Yr - 4	Yr - 3	Yr - 2	Yr - 1
abdominoplasty	81,200	92,000	102,400	110,800	124,400	129,700
augmentation mammoplasty	140,300	145,900	182,700	196,700	220,100	228,200
blepharoplasty	180,200	188,300	191,600	199,400	212,400	218,200
Botox	71,900	79,925	117,875	124,300	132,800	138,300
breast Implant Removal	31,200	35,200	38,400	42,500	47,400	59,200
endobrow lift	0	32,800	38,800	41,000	48,100	52,300
chemical Peel	0	38,400	67,200	73,000	80,800	88,000
dermabrasion	0	55,000	59,200	66,000	73,000	84,400
facial implant	25,300	29,400	60,900	73,500	76,400	69,300
inj Collagen	26,000	33,750	39,250	48,300	55,100	57,300
inj Radiance	28,800	30,625	37,500	42,200	49,800	51,800
inj Restylane	31,875	36,000	47,400	54,600	48,000	54,800
laser hair removal	0	5,400	9,450	21,600	22,800	23,200
laser resurface	0	48,600	66,800	77,000	82,500	84,000
lip augmentation	0	17,600	42,800	51,400	59,000	72,400
liposuction	304,700	322,000	325,900	322,900	324,000	328,400
mastopexy	184,200	197,600	223,700	227,600	232,000	239,600
reduction mammoplasty	92,400	72,600	88,800	91,300	103,300	99,000
rhinoplasty	392,800	421,200	422,200	450,800	458,900	467,500
rhytidectomy	688,200	702,200	765,000	770,300	781,200	784,300
sclerotherapy	0	19,250	28,700	72,600	81,000	83,400
Totals	2,279,075	2,603,750	2,956,575	3,157,800	3,313,000	3,413,300
Revenue Increase over previous year	20%	14.25%	13.55%	6.80%	4.90%	3.03

Regency Plastic Surgery
Expense Report
Office 6 (Oakdale)

Category	YR-6	YR-5	YR-4	YR-3	YR-2	YR-1
Rent	215,728	210,600	210,600	210,600	221,700	221,700
Non-professional Compensation	104,417	138,478	139,456	138,174	141,002	163,122
Office Admin	54,123	41,879	43,458	42,745	48,415	51,471
Advertising	120,000	124,000	132,000	134,000	138,000	144,000
Professional Compensation	1,000,000	1,200,000	1,300,000	1,400,000	1,500,000	1,700,000
Equipment and Supplies	144,200	132,500	128,900	130,200	136,200	140,000
Totals	1,638,468	1,847,457	1,954,414	2,055,719	2,185,317	2,420,293
Gross Profit	640607	756293	1002161	1102081	1127683	993007
Gross Profit Margin	28%	29.00%	34.00%	35%	34%	29%

Exhibit 8

Regency "Look of Love" advertisement

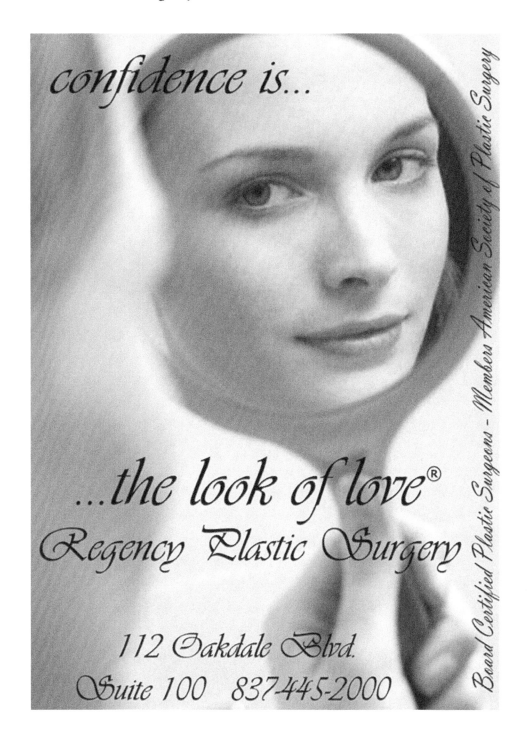

Exhibit 9

Connelly, Robert

From: Diana Segan, MD [dsegan@regencyplastics.nita]
Sent: November 17, YR-5 9:40 p.m.
To: Connelly, Robert
Subject: Dr. Love

Thanks, Bob. I'm much relieved.

Diana

From: Connelly, Robert [rconnelly@w&c.mds.nita]
Sent: November 17, YR-5 9:05 p.m.
To: Diana Segan, MD
Subject: Dr. Love

Diana

Given our anticipated upscale, sophisticated patient population, I can't imagine that anyone will think that Stan Love is associated with Regency.

As to competition, although we and Stan offer many of the same services, I highly doubt that his rather shoestring operation will take any prospective patients away from Regency. We'll have a much classier operation, in a much more desirable location (and you know what they say about location). If anything, we'll wind up with some of his prospective patients, not the reverse. But given the differences in the quality of our services, our higher fee structure, and the tone or our advertising, I doubt there will be any confusion.

I hope this allays your concerns.

Bob

From: Diana Segan, MD [dsegan@regencyplastics.nita]
Sent: November 16, YR-5 11:55 p.m.
To: Connelly, Robert
Subject: Dr. Love

Bob

I enjoyed meeting with you and Carl and I thank you for your hospitality. Please send my special thanks to Mary Jane for the exceptional meal. She really works wonders with veal chops.

We should complete our due diligence very soon. I am quite optimistic that everything will be fine, and that you'll be joining the Regency family in January. I have one niggling concern, however, and it has to do with Dr. Love in Central City and his low-rent commercials.

We are very protective of "The Look of Love" and I want to make sure that, despite the similarity of our slogans, no one will think that Dr. Love has anything to do with Regency. I'm happy to compete with him, but I don't want to be confused with him. Because you know the Central City area medical landscape, I need your reassurance.

Best,

Diana

Diana Segan, M.D.

President

Regency Plastic Surgery, PC

341 E. 66th Street

New York, NY

regencyplastics.nita

Exhibit 10

You too can have...

The Love Look

Stanley Love MD, PC
Dermatology, Cosmetic Surgery
For an appointment call 1-800-LOVLOOK

...*you owe it to yourself!*

Home   Staff   Services   New Patients   Contact Us

Stanley Love MD, PC is not associated with any other medical practice.

"Our Staff:"

Office Manager Bobbi

Stanley Love, M.D., P.C.

Nurse Debby

Home   Staff   Services   New Patients   Contact Us

Stanley Love MD, PC is not associated with any other medical practice.

"How to find us"

Dr. Stanley Love, M.D., P.C.
Dermatology and Cosmetic Surgery
"The Love Look"
3345 Richton
Central City, NITA

Hours by Appointment
1-800-LOVLOOK
(1-800-568-5665)

Home   Staff   Services   New Patients   Contact Us

Stanley Love MD, PC is not associated with any other medical practice.

Exhibit 11

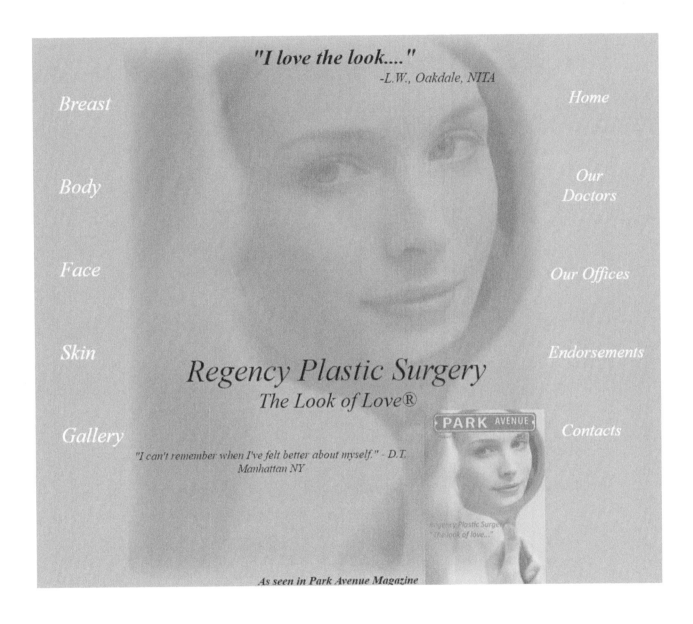

Our Doctors

Our New York Office
Diana Segen, MD
Board Certified: General Surgery
Plastic Surgery

Dale Trimble, MD
Board Certified: General Surgery
Plastic Surgery
Fellow: American Academy of Cosmetic Surgery

Amidsa Kanoun, MD
Board Certified: Plastic Surgery

Randall Jones, MD
Board Certified: Plastic Surgery

Home

Our
Doctors

Our Offices

Breast

Body

Face

Skin

Gallery

Endorsements

Contacts

Our Stamford Office
Hal Woodward, MD
Board Certified: Plastic Surgery
Fellow: American Academy of Cosmetic Surgery

Rachel Levin, MD
Board Certified: General Surgery
Plastic Surgery

Rebecca Goldman, MD
Board Certified: Plastic Surgery

Our Saddle River Office
Joseph Rossi, MD
Board Certified: General Surgery
Plastic Surgery

Hannah Kowaleczyk, MD
Board Certified: Plastic Surgery
Plastic Surgery
Fellow: American Academy of Cosmetic Surgery

Our Buckhead Office
Paula Grace, MD
Board Certified: Plastic Surgery
Fellow: American Academy of Cosmetic Surgery

Jeff Laszlo, MD
Board Certified: Plastic Surgery

Our Naples Office
Ivy Moss, MD
Board Certified: General Surgery
Plastic Surgery
Fellow: American Academy of Cosmetic Surgery

Denzel Abelman, MD
Board Certified: General Surgery
Plastic Surgery
Fellow: American Academy of Cosmetic Surgery

Lisa Almasi, MD
Board Certified: Plastic Surgery

Our Oakdale Office
Carl Waters, MD
Board Certified: General Surgery
Plastic Surgery

Robert Connelly, MD
Board Certified: General Surgery
Plastic Surgery

Our Offices

Breast

Home

Our New York Office
341 E. 66th Street
New York, NY 10065
(201) 555-3939

Our Stamford Office
2975 Summer Street
Stamford, CT 06901
(203) 555-8800

Body

Our
Doctors

Our Saddle River Office
7 Pearl Court
Allendale, NJ 07401
(908) 555-4589

Our Buckhead Office
843 Baldwin Dairy Road
Buckhead, OH 30625
(404) 555-1234

Face

Our Offices

Our Naples Office
2727 Pine Ridge Rd.
Naples, FL 34109
(239) 555-4292

Our Oakdale Office
3700 Summit Dr.
Oakdale, NT 80148
(721) 555-6482

Skin

Endorsements

Gallery

Contacts

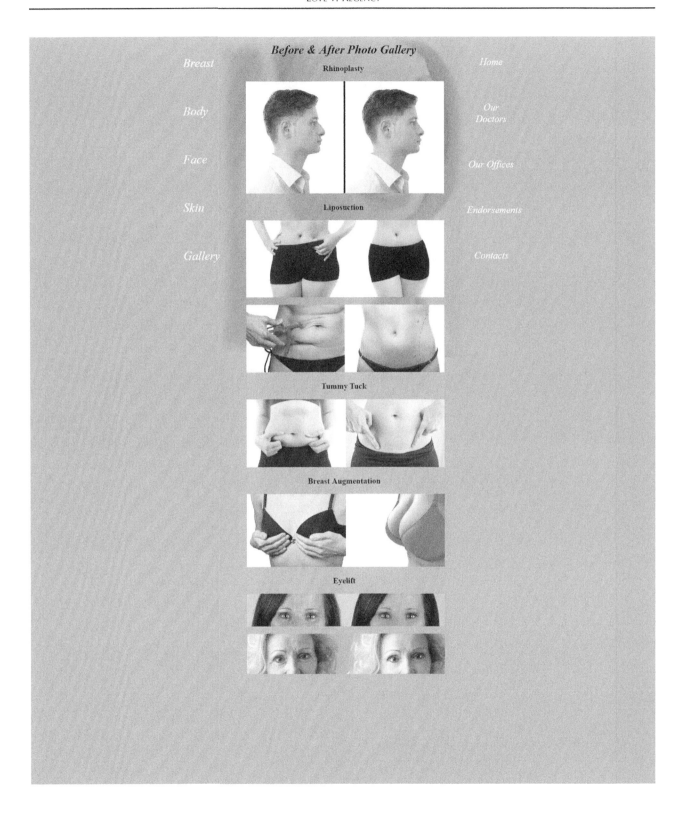

Endorsements

Breast

Home

"I have so much more confidence now. I wish I had invested in myself years ago."

- M. P., Trenton, NJ

"There are no words for how thankful I am to have found you. My husband can't keep his eyes—or his hands—off me."

Body

Our
Doctors

- D. K., Long Island, NY

"My liposuction far exceeded my expectations! I went from a size 12 to a size 6! Whenever anyone asks how I did it, I refer them to you."

- B. C., Marietta, GA

Face

Our Offices

"You work miracles."

- P. R., Schenectady, NY

"Thanks to you, I look and feel so much better about myself."

- M. W., Naples, FL

Skin

Endorsements

"I've had several different procedures, and I wouldn't dream of going anywhere else. Every time I knew I would be taken care of. It's worth the drive to go to Regency. I trust all of them."

H. K., Providence, RI

Gallery

Contacts

"I couldn't be happier with the results."

- G. L., Central City, NI

Exhibit 12

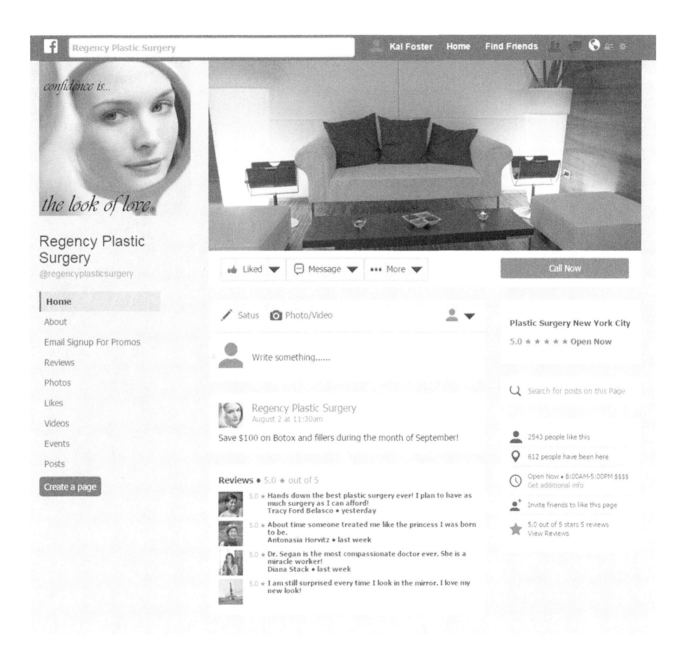

Appendices

SUMMARY OF APPLICABLE LAW

The Nita State Supreme Court has repeatedly held that usage in this state provides a common law trademark in an unregistered name or slogan, so long as the name or slogan is "fanciful," as opposed to merely descriptive. Thus, the Supreme Court has upheld "Purple Passion" as a common law trademarked name for grape soda pop, while denying common law trademark protection to "Good Old Grape Pop."

The State Supreme Court has held that once one acquires a common law trademark in a name or slogan in this state, that right cannot by defeated by another person's later registration of the name or slogan with the U.S. Patent and Trademark Office (USPTO). Such registration may provide the owner with rights in other states, but it does not affect a prior common law trademark in this state. On the other hand, once someone registers a name or slogan with the USPTO, no one else can thereafter acquire new common law trademark protection in any state.

State law provides that one whose common law trademark has been infringed can obtain an injunction against the infringer. The test for infringement is whether the defendant's use of a name or slogan is likely (probable) to cause confusion in the public's mind between the plaintiff's goods/services and the defendant's. The Supreme Court has held that the following factors should be considered in determining the likelihood of confusion:

1. Strength (distinctiveness) of the plaintiff's name or slogan;

2. Relatedness of the goods or services provided by the parties;

3. Similarity of the names or slogans;

4. Evidence of actual confusion;

5. Similarity of marketing channels used;

6. Likely degree of purchaser care in selecting the goods/services in question;

7. Defendant's intent in selecting the name or slogan (e.g., whether defendant intended to capitalize on the plaintiff's mark);

8. Likelihood of either party's expansion of product/service lines to more closely resemble the other party's.

The Supreme Court has held that, in determining whether to grant a preliminary injunction, the trial court should consider the following factors:

1. Plaintiff's likelihood of success on the merits;

2. Irreparable injury to the plaintiff if the injunction is not granted (this is presumed on a preliminary finding of likely trademark infringement);

3. Substantial harm to others if the injunction is, or is not, granted; and

4. Whether the public interest is served by the grant of an injunction.

A plaintiff may also obtain past and future damages for infringement. The measure of damages is the loss to the plaintiff, or profit to the defendant, whichever is greater.

A plaintiff can obtain treble damages and attorneys' fees where the trier of fact finds willful infringement. "Willful" is defined as infringement by a defendant who has actual knowledge that his actions are infringing on the plaintiff's common law trademark.

The statute of limitations for a damage claim in this state is six years. The doctrine of laches applies to a claim for an injunction. The Supreme Court has held that a court of equity, in determining whether the plaintiff is barred by laches, should consider, but is not bound by, the statute of limitations that would be applicable to a damage claim. One is barred by laches if he delays an unreasonable time in filing suit to enforce his rights, and the defendant is damaged by the delay. Unreasonableness is decided on a case-specific basis.

MEDICAL TERMINOLOGY

Abdominoplasty – "tummy tuck" surgery

Augmentation Mammoplasty – breast enlargement

Blepharoplasty – eyelid surgery to remove excess sagging skin

Botox – injection of dilute botulinum neurotoxin that causes partial facial muscle paralysis with resultant decrease in wrinkles of skin overlying paralyzed muscles

Chemical Peel – chemically induced shedding of the outmost layer of the skin (this is the outermost layer of dead skin cells)

Dermabrasion – procedure to remove skin imperfections by abrasion or "sanding"

Endobrow Lift – facelift involving the forehead

Facial Implant – placement of artificial material to enhance "bone structure," usually placed in the nose or chin

Filler Injections – injections of biologic material to fill unsightly depressions in the skin. This includes collagen, *Radiance* and *Restylane*

Laser Hair Removal – procedure using a laser to destroy unwanted hair follicles

Laser Resurfacing – similar to Dermabrasion, except that a laser is used to remove skin imperfections instead of a "sanding" technique

Lip Augmentation – injection of fat or other biologic material into lips

Liposuction – vacuum procedure to remove subcutaneous fat

Mastopexy – breast surgery to correct sagging

Reduction Mammoplasty – surgery to reduce breast size

Rhinoplasty – surgery to reshape the nose

Rhytidectomy – facelift surgery

Spider Veins – small dilated (varicose) veins which have the appearance of spiders directly under the skin

Sclerotherapy – injection of a chemical irritant into spider veins, causing the veins to close and disappear

Spider Vein Laser – laser beam used to destroy spider veins

Medical/Surgical Credentialing

Dermatologists are physicians who complete residencies in dermatology and specialize in the care of the skin. To become certified by the American Board of Dermatology, one must complete medical school, internship, and an approved residency in dermatology that lasts for three years beyond the internship year. One must also pass the certification exam given by the American Board of Dermatology. Dermatology residency typically includes training in a limited number of surgical procedures, some of which may be described as "cosmetic" in nature. Some dermatologists elect to undergo a dermatologic surgery fellowship. This additional year of training provides experience in cosmetic and cancer-related skin surgery. Upon completion, they are qualified to practice dermatologic surgery.

The American Academy of Dermatology accredits training programs in dermatology. It also confers fellowship status based, in part, on certification by the American Board of Dermatology. The American Board of Dermatology certifies dermatologists by administering an oral and written examination. The American Board of Dermatology is recognized by the American Board of Medical Specialties.

Dermatology—Years of Internship/Residency: 4

Plastic Surgeons are physicians who complete residencies in plastic surgery and specialize in surgery for body modification and reconstruction. To become certified by the American Board of Plastic Surgery, one must complete medical school, internship, and an additional three years of general surgery residency. A minimum of two years of plastic surgical residency are also required, prior to passing a certification examination given by the American Board of Plastic Surgery. Plastic surgeons typically perform a larger number of more complex cosmetic surgical procedures, in addition to the restorative surgery they perform. These restorative surgeries are performed, for example, on cancer or burn patients.

The American Board of Surgery certifies general surgeons, while the American Board of Plastic Surgery certifies plastic surgeons. Both administer oral and written exams for certification. Both are recognized by the American Board of Medical Specialties. The American Society of Plastic Surgeons affords membership only to fully qualified plastic surgeons.

Plastic Surgery—Years of Internship/Residency: 6 To 8

Cosmetic Surgeons are physicians who have a strong interest in cosmetic surgery. There are no formal requirements to use the term "cosmetic" surgeon. The American Board of Cosmetic Surgery offers credentialing to physicians who complete residencies in dermatology, ear, nose, and throat surgery, as well as other specialties. These physicians may choose to become board certified in cosmetic surgery by completing an approved additional fellowship year in cosmetic surgery and up to 300 hours of continuing medical education in topics of relevance to cosmetic surgery (depending on other certification). Until 2008, physicians could obtain board certification by performing at least 1,000 cosmetic surgical procedures, without completing a fellowship year. This pathway was eliminated in August 2008, in favor of an accredited fellowship. After completing these educational requirements, board candidates must pass a certification exam given by the American Board of Cosmetic Surgery. The American Academy of Cosmetic Surgery awards fellowship status to physicians who have completed at least one hundred cosmetic surgical procedures. This "fellow" designation is independent of board certification in cosmetic surgery.

The American Board of Cosmetic Surgery certifies cosmetic surgeons following a one year fellowship (or completion of 1,000 procedures before 2008). The American Board of Cosmetic Surgery is not recognized by the American Board of Medical Specialties. The American Academy of Cosmetic Surgery accredits training programs in cosmetic surgery, and bestows the designation "Fellow of the American Academy of Cosmetic Surgery" after completion of one hundred cosmetic surgical procedures (board certification not required).

COSMETIC SURGERY–YEARS OF INTERNSHIP/ RESIDENCY: VARIABLE DEPENDING ON OTHER CERTIFICATION

Jury Instructions

1. The law you are to apply to this case is contained in these instructions, and it is your duty to follow them. You must consider them as a whole, and not pick out one or some instructions and disregard others.

2. Sympathy or prejudice must not influence your decision.

3. I have not meant to indicate any opinion as to the facts by my rulings, conduct, or remarks during the trial. But if you think I have, you should disregard it because you are the sole judges of the facts.

4. You shall consider all of the evidence bearing on any fact without regard to which party produced the evidence.

5. A fact may be proven directly by a witness or indirectly by other facts or circumstances from which it reasonably follows according to the common experience of mankind. This indirect evidence is called circumstantial evidence, and it should be considered by you in the same manner as direct evidence.

6. In determining which witnesses you will believe and what weight you will give to their testimony, you may take into account each witness's ability and opportunity to observe, his or her memory, manner while testifying, and any interest, bias, or prejudice he or she may have.

7. Plaintiffs claim that, because they were using "The Love Look" as their slogan before defendant registered "The Look of Love" as its slogan, the plaintiffs acquired a common law trademark in "The Love Look" which is superior in this state to the defendant's later, federally registered trademark of "The Look of Love." In connection with this claim, Plaintiffs have the burden of proving, by a preponderance of the evidence, that the slogan, "The Love Look," as applied to Dr. Love's cosmetic surgery, is not merely descriptive of his surgery, but is a fanciful slogan—that is, a slogan used in an imaginative way. If you find that plaintiffs have met their burden of proof, then you must find that their trademark is superior to (e.g., takes precedence over) the defendant's trademark in this state.

8. Plaintiffs also claim that defendant infringed on its trademark rights to the slogan, "The Love Look." In connection with this claim, plaintiffs have the burden of proving, by a preponderance of the evidence, that defendant's use of "The Look of Love" would probably cause confusion in the public's mind between plaintiffs' and defendant's cosmetic surgery practices. In your determination of this issue, you should consider the following, to the extent that you find they are supported by the evidence:

    a) The distinctiveness of the plaintiffs' slogan, "The Love Look";

    b) The similarity of the services provided by the parties;

    c) Any similarity of the parties' slogans;

    d) Any evidence of actual confusion;

    e) Any similarity of marketing channels;

    f) The likelihood of purchaser care in selecting a cosmetic surgery provider;

    g) Whether defendant intended to capitalize on plaintiffs' slogan; and

h) Any evidence of defendant's expansion of its cosmetic surgery services to more closely resemble plaintiffs'.

9. Plaintiffs also claim, and have the burden of proving by a preponderance of the evidence, that they have been damaged by defendant's infringement of plaintiffs' "The Love Look" slogan.

10. Your verdict will be for the plaintiffs if they prove that:

a) "The Love Look," as applied to Dr. Love's cosmetic surgery, is not merely descriptive of his surgery, but is a fanciful slogan (used in an imaginative way); and

b) Defendant infringed on its trademark rights to the slogan, "The Love Look"; and

c) The plaintiffs have been damaged by defendant's infringement of plaintiffs' "The Love Look" slogan.

Your verdict will be for the defendant if plaintiffs fail to prove any of these elements.

11. If you find that the plaintiffs are entitled to damages, you should determine the amount of money that will fairly compensate them for the following elements of damage, as proved by the evidence:

a) Plaintiffs' past lost profits or defendant's profits from its infringement (whichever is greater), and

b) Plaintiff's future lost profits.

12. If your verdict is for the plaintiffs, you must also determine whether plaintiffs have proved, by a preponderance of the evidence, that defendant's infringement was willful. The term "willful" means that defendant had actual knowledge that it was infringing on the plaintiff's trademark rights to the slogan, "The Love Look."

13. I will furnish you with a form for your verdict. Please fill in the appropriate blank(s) when ____ of you agree to the answer.

STATE COURT OF NITA
COUNTY OF NITA

STANLEY LOVE, MD and	)	
STANLEY LOVE, MD, PC,	)	
	)	
Plaintiffs,	)	
	)	
vs.	)	CIVIL NO. YR–1–CV–96369
	)	
REGENCY PLASTIC SURGERY,	)	
	)	
Defendant.	)	
	)	

VERDICT FORM
[trial on liability and damages]

We find as follows:

QUESTION #1: Is the slogan, "The Love Look," as applied to Dr. Love's cosmetic surgery, not merely descriptive of his surgery, but a fanciful slogan?

      ANSWER: _____ [Yes or No]

If your answer is "no," do not answer any further questions.

QUESTION #2: Did the defendant infringe on the plaintiffs' "The Love Look" slogan?

      ANSWER: _____ [Yes or No]

If your answer is "no," do not answer any further questions.

QUESTION #3: Were the plaintiffs damaged by the defendant's infringement of the plaintiffs' "The Love Look" slogan?

      ANSWER: _____ [Yes or No]

If your answer is "no," do not answer any further questions.

QUESTION #4: What are the plaintiffs' damages for:

      Past lost profits or the defendant's infringement profits $_____

      Future lost profits $_____

QUESTION #5: Was the defendant's infringement of "The Love Look" slogan willful?

      ANSWER: _____ [Yes or No]

                Signed,

                Jury Foreperson

STATE COURT OF NITA
COUNTY OF NITA

STANLEY LOVE, MD and)
STANLEY LOVE, MD, PC,)
)
Plaintiffs,)
)
vs.)   CIVIL NO. YR–1–CV–96369
)
REGENCY PLASTIC SURGERY,)
)
Defendant.)
)

VERDICT FORM
[trial on liability only]

We find as follows:

QUESTION #1: Is the slogan, "The Love Look," as applied to Dr. Love's cosmetic surgery, not merely descriptive of his surgery, but a fanciful slogan?

> **ANSWER:** _____ [Yes or No]

If your answer is "no," do not answer any further questions.

QUESTION #2: Did the defendant infringe on the plaintiffs' "The Love Look" slogan?

> **ANSWER:** _____ [Yes or No]

If your answer is "no," do not answer any further questions.

QUESTION #3: Were the plaintiffs damaged by the defendant's infringement of the plaintiffs' "The Love Look" slogan?

> **ANSWER:** _____ [Yes or No]

Signed,

Jury Foreperson

IMPEACHMENT EXERCISES

1. Assume that Dr. Love testified on direct exam that the first time he considered suing Regency was last year [Yr-1] when his cosmetic surgery revenues continued to decline. Impeach him from his deposition.

2. Assume Dr. Love testified on direct examination: "I left a detailed message for Dr. Waters on his answering machine that Regency was unfairly trading on my slogan." Impeach him from his deposition.

3. Assume that J. Anderson testified on direct exam that "The Look of Love" slogan played absolutely no part in his decision to have surgery at Regency. Impeach him from his deposition.

4. Assume that C. Delp testified on direct exam that when she mistakenly called Regency's office, she specifically asked for an appointment with Dr. Love. Impeach her from her deposition.

5. Assume that Dr. Segan testified on direct exam that she absolutely did not recall Exhibit 4 when she was planning the Oakdale office or when she gave the go ahead to use The Look of Love campaign in the Central City area. Impeach her from her deposition.

6. Assume Dr. Segan testified on Direct Examination: "The reason Dr. Yale and I limited our practice to cosmetic surgery was first and foremost because we were emotionally burnt out after treating badly deformed patients." Impeach her from her deposition..

Made in the USA
Middletown, DE
08 September 2024

60585463R00084